MW00617588

Toxic Sons- and Daughters-in-Law

Untangling Difficult Relationships

Other books by Doyle Roth include:

Oops! I Forgot My Wife:
A Story of Commitment as Marriage and Self-Centeredness Collide

Oops! I Forgot My Wife Discussion Guide
(Co-authored with Paul Santhouse)

Oops! We Forgot the Kids:
A Story of Relationships as Parenting and Self-Centeredness Collide

Toxic Sons- and Daughters-in-Law

Untangling Difficult Relationships

Doyle Roth

Toxic Sons- and Daughters-in-Law: Untangling Difficult Relationships
ISBN-10: 0936083484
ISBN-13: 9780936083483
Copyright © 2019 by Doyle Roth. All rights reserved.

Typesetting and Cover Design: Bryana Mansfield

Unless otherwise indicated, Scripture quotations are taken from the New
American Standard Bible® (NASB).
Copyright © 1960, 1962, 1963, 1968, 1971, 1972, 1973, 1975, 1977, 1995
by The Lockman Foundation. Used by permission. www.Lockman.org.

Scripture quotations marked NKJV are taken from the New King James
Version®. Copyright © 1982 by Thomas Nelson. Used by permission.
All rights reserved.

Printed in the United States of America
First Printing 2019

To receive a free catalog of books published by Lewis and Roth Publishers,
please call toll free 800-477-3239 or visit *www.lewisandroth.com.* If you are
calling from outside the United States, please call 719-494-1800.

Lewis and Roth Publishers
P. O. Box 469
Littleton, Colorado 80160

Contents

Conclusion

Dedication

How can I express in such a small space the appreciation I feel for those who have made this book a reality? The most important people are dead, buried, and enjoying eternal life in heaven. Robert M. and Mabel G. Lewis became my father- and mother-in-law in 1963, when I married their daughter. They were a wonderful example of in-laws who unconditionally loved the unlovely … me in particular. I praise God for their patience, and willingness to "bite their tongues" and allow time for me to grow up emotionally and mature spiritually.

Looking back now over nearly fifty-five years of married life, I'm thankful for my lifelong partner, Nancy. Only a sovereign God would know that she was best for me. During our early years of marriage, she alone could navigate the perilous terrain between an immature husband and her parents (my father- and mother-in-law).

I want to say thanks to the many wonderful parents who have poured out their hurts and frustrations in my counseling office because of a difficult son- or daughter-in-law. Their examples of facing faith and family challenges with courage and Christlikeness have set the bar high. The heartache, frustration, disappointment, and often failure in such relationships have created a garden of trials where their spiritual lives have been watered and pruned, making them blossom into something of great beauty and worthy of admiration. These parents have learned firsthand that "tribulation brings about perseverance; and perseverance, proven character; and proven character, hope" (Romans 5:3–4).

Finally, thanks to the many terrific sons- and daughters-in-law who've been great examples of kindness and compassion to your spouse's parents. You understand the value of family relationships and have been like Ruth (Ruth 1:16–17), who loved and chose to serve her mother-in-law with great personal sacrifice. You have understood and applied the wonderful commandment with a promise in Exodus 20:12: "Honor your father and your mother, that your days may be prolonged in the land." I hold you in high esteem because you are very rare indeed.

Last, but certainly not least, are those many friends who've commented, corrected, and encouraged me to finish this book. A special thanks to Lisa Corbett who was first to edit the manuscript and bring a cowboy's writing style into a smooth and readable text. Lisa, you were so helpful.

Introduction

Do you have any idea how many parents deal with a difficult son- or daughter-in-law? Are you aware of the pain and suffering brought on by these insensitive, childish, self-absorbed in-laws? Here we'll consider one of the most disturbing and distressing issues a parent can face.

Let me start by telling you this book is not about bad fathers- or mothers-in-law. There are enough books on that subject to fill a few landfills. They include frightening stories about fathers-in-law who are angry, distant, drunk, controlling, couch potatoes, or mothers-in-law who are manipulative, bossy, critical, or overly sensitive. While I readily admit there are plenty of those kinds of in-laws, this book is different. *Toxic Sons- and Daughters-in-Law* is about abusive, problematic, controlling people our children marry and drag into their family of origin—namely your family.

This book has been incubating in my head and heart for many years. I've watched as many families struggled under the sinful and childish behavior of a son-

or daughter-in-law who is a total "pain in the neck." However, in the last few years, this book has taken on new life as I've counseled numerous families who've been challenged by an angry, egotistical, irrational, oppressive son- or daughter-in-law. This has become epidemic in our "me first," narcissistic society.

Toxic Sons- and Daughters-in-Law recaps the tragedy faced by families in this situation. You'll read the gruesome details of families suffering through distressing relationships with troublesome sons- or daughters-in-law. Do not underestimate the seriousness of the emotional and spiritual battle each family confronts every day on this stress-filled journey of living with a difficult son- or daughter-in-law. I've been so impressed with how these families have managed to cope and survive. They've endured because they refuse to give up on their child or compromise their own spiritual integrity. And yet they're deeply troubled by the withdrawal of their son or daughter under the negative influence of their son- or daughter-in-law.

The stories in this book are true (although I've changed the names to protect the identities of the individuals involved). But the families you'll read about are not what you might think. They aren't overbearing, dysfunctional families attempting to run their children's lives. In fact, they are the complete opposite, representing high-quality, well-balanced, loving Christian dads and moms. They've just been blindsided by a guy or gal who's married to their son or daughter.

This might be an appropriate time for a personal disclaimer. I've been a counselor for over four decades. My interest in counseling started while working with teenagers as a church youth worker. As a church pastor, ministry leader and business owner, there was a gradual shift from working with teenagers to helping adults deal with more complex issues: marital and parenting problems, emotional struggles, business and financial matters. I've never had any formal training in counseling or psychology. My education has consisted of self-study through many helpful resources, primarily the Bible, and thousands of hours of experience in my counseling office with people seeking guidance for just about every conceivable situation. Over the years, I have gained a wealth of information through both experience and study. I have had the joy of counseling others and helping them apply insights to their own individual lives and situations. I consider myself to be the greatest beneficiary of all these different encounters and pray that my time with individuals and families has been as beneficial to them. It's a great joy to be in a position where you have the opportunity to invest your time and experience in the lives of others and I thank God for allowing me this great privilege.

I'm an old cowboy who's convinced all emotions and behaviors come under the guidelines and scrutiny of Holy Scripture. I believe God has the final say on life and godliness through His Word, the Holy Bible, and I make no apology for my position. I guess I'm the kind of counselor you either love for my "no nonsense" biblical approach, or you dislike for being "too religious" or lacking sensitivity. Either way, I want to assure you that I do care about your family.

One more disclaimer: I think most people would consider me a loving, patient, thoughtful, and respectful cowboy… most of the time. I also think my wife, children, and extended family members would agree… most of the time. But they would also tell you that if I believe someone is being unjustly treated, hurt intentionally, disrespected, or abused, I can get pretty ornery—defending, protecting, and speaking very directly with righteous, biblical anger. You will likely sense that as you read on. If you're easily offended by directness, then you probably should give this book to the Goodwill Store and not read further. If you're not easily offended, then continue to read. You will eventually understand how deeply troubled I am over this subject.

In *Toxic Sons- and Daughters-in-Law*, we will look to the Bible for guidance, strength, and assurance. If you're one of those struggling parents, I'll try to equip you biblically with insights and means to tap into God's strength while you're trying to keep your cool, avoid murder, stay out of jail, and maintain a Christian testimony.

In this book, I'll challenge sons- and daughters-in-law to come to terms with the emotional hurt, frustration, fear, disappointment, and anxiety their fathers- and mothers-in-law endure because of their destructive attitudes. Spiritual maturity and biblical application, including unconditional love and mutual respect, are imperative for families to stay together.

But these must come from the sons- and daughters-in-law as well as the parents.

Toxic Sons- and Daughters-in-Law will be a good resource for dads and moms, counselors, elders, and pastors to utilize for discussion during all pre-marital programs. It would also be helpful for parents to read this book in preparation for what can be a very difficult transition. Remember, an ounce of prevention is better than a pound of cure. It is my prayer God will bring renewal to hurting relationships through repentance, humility, and mutual honor on the part of everyone involved.

Part One
Biblical Perspectives

CHAPTER ONE

When An Outsider Joins Your Family

The best way to prepare readers for *Toxic Sons- and Daughters-in-Law* is by telling my own story. Some 55 years ago, I was a problematic son-in-law. It all began in 1963 when Nancy and I married. For the first several years, I was a very immature and unreasonable son-in-law. Allow yourself to imagine what it must have been like for my father- and mother-in-law to realize they were permanently attached to a self-centered, self-righteous, self-willed, highly opinionated, and very immature "Christian." I judged, condemned, and found fault with just about everything they did or tried to do for us and our children. How they tolerated my selfish behavior is beyond my comprehension.

Here's the kicker: should Nancy agree with her parents on a particular matter, I interpreted her support of her parents as a lack of submission to me and a defection from our marital vows. My dear Nancy was caught between the kindness of her parents and the selfishness and insecurity of her husband. My in-laws were on the outside looking in, walking on eggshells, and dodging minefields, not knowing what to expect next.

Oh, how it must have troubled them to see how I treated them and their wonderful daughter! Why they didn't send some thugs to knock me around a bit, I'll never fully understand. Through the years, my in-laws continued to be patient, persevering, flexible, understanding, helpful, and gracious. And, by God's grace, I gradually matured …somewhat. Looking back at more than fifty of years of marriage, I thank God for them and for His Word that held us together, encouraged my spiritual growth, and gave me a more balanced appreciation for my wonderful in-laws.

When my children grew up and I acquired sons- and daughters-in-law of my own, the light finally came on in my brain: My father- and mother-in-law had put up with me during those difficult times for their daughter's sake. In other words, they tolerated my foolishness and refused to make waves in order to not lose their relationship with Nancy. That's critical for parents to understand, and that they should not forget.

The issue of toxic sons- or daughters-in-law has become a point of particular interest to me in recent counseling experiences. In the last few years, over forty couples have come to my office for counsel about their sons- or daughters-in-law. Let me explain the general situation. For the moment, let's think of sons- and daughters-in-law as outsiders, not because they are of lesser importance to a family but because they are not part of the original family unit. This is an important distinction to remember. The outsider joins the original family unit through a marriage.

Many families are greatly blessed by the addition of these outsiders. Others are not so blessed. Some of these outsiders are toxic, abusive, controlling, insecure, or manipulative. They are egotistical and lack compassion for their fathers- and mothers-in-law and even brothers- or sisters-in-law in the original family unit. This scenario is very disturbing, and it seems to be on the rise among both Christian and non-Christian families.

The painful stories about toxic sons- and daughters-in-law I've encountered are the real reason behind this book. I've been keeping track of these families and praying with them for years. Counseling with parents who are in this pickle has been life-changing for me. I feel their emotional pain and pent-up anger and frustration but I also see their courage, concern, patience, and perseverance. This has been encouraging to me in my personal walk with the Lord, as well as in my counseling ministry.

The families whose stories you'll read have some important things in common. First, the dads and moms from each family are very fine Christ-followers who have labored to raise their children with an appreciation for biblical instruction. Each family is involved in and committed to church life and service to others. Generally speaking, they've maintained healthy relationships with their son or daughter leading up to the wedding and the addition of the outsider to the original family unit. Most would consider them model families. I mention this because you might be inclined to think the problem lies with the father- or mother-in-law being controlling, demanding, and having unrealistic expectations. I can assure you that isn't the case.

In addition, each family also shares a particular heartache that puts them on my radar. They have a son- or daughter-in-law who's a genuinely toxic individual. Consequently, what was once a loving, healthy family unit has been thrown into a terrifying tailspin since the outsider joined.

There's not a single family on my list that doesn't understand Genesis 2:24: "For this reason a man shall leave his father and his mother, and be joined to his wife." In fact, the parents desire that their children marry and build a life of their own. More than that, they want them to experience the independence and freedom that comes from "leaving and cleaving" to their new spouse.

But in the case of these families, the son or daughter marries a person who is insecure, headstrong, controlling, manipulative, or just insensitive and lacking compassion.

Their son- or daughter-in-law may even have severe emotional or mental health issues that went undetected during the dating, courtship, and engagement process. This individual brings all kinds of turbulence into the family unit, causing all hopes and dreams of happy relationships with a great son- or daughter-in-law to evaporate quickly.

The stories I share in this book are just a small sampling of many families who have this shared experience. As you read on, you'll get an inside look at the hurt parents go through in these situations. You'll read what it's like for a dad and mom to suppress their anger and live with rejection, ill treatment, false accusations, and lack of respect. All the while, these godly parents accept the hurt with humility and Christlikeness. If you have an ounce of empathy, you might feel your throat tighten while you try to grapple with the injustice of it all. I encourage you to weep with them, pray for them, and understand the difficulties they face.

My purpose in writing this book is fourfold:

- To explain the growing problem of toxic sons- or daughters-in-law through real life stories.

- To provide encouragement and counsel for those suffering at the hands of a toxic son- or daughter-in-law. I want you to know that you're not alone! I'll try to answer the question, "What can we do to untangle this mess?"

- To expose the abusive behavior of the son- or daughter-in-law who rejects, criticizes, ostracizes, or blames their father- or mother-in-law for desiring a relationship with their child and their child's family. Such abusive attitudes are very sick and selfish.

- To provide a premarital counseling tool for future sons- or daughters-in-law which will exhort them and teach them God's desire that they honor, respect, love, and sometimes forgive their spouse's parents. This requires intentional effort on the part of the son- or daughter-in-law. It isn't an automatic emotion that arrives at the conclusion of the wedding ceremony.

There is a growing epidemic of these disturbing behaviors and relationships among both Christian and non-Christian families. It has been on my heart to address this issue and to encourage parents who are facing such difficult circumstances. It won't be easy, but it's a necessary journey. So, find a comfy place to sit, a cool drink, some snacks, and read on.

CHAPTER TWO

Scripture Is Our Manual

I just bought a pressure washer. It came in a box with a bucket full of disconnected parts, and an owner's manual that explains in detail everything I need to know in order to squeeze every ounce of pleasure out of my new toy.

Generally, men don't read owner's manuals. We typically see them as backup instructions in the event our assembly gets goofed up and the pressure washer ends up working like an oversized hair dryer. Well, I decided to break with tradition and follow the assembly instructions in the manual. Consequently, my new toy works perfectly, and I learned something about owner's manuals. They generally cover four very necessary categories of instruction.

1. **Design.** The manual is designed by engineers or architects who know how it works best and who explain the design for the user.

2. **Purpose.** The manual explains that the washer was made for the purpose of using high pressure water to clean engines, concrete, decks, tractors, etc.

3. **Warnings.** These tell you what you shouldn't do with the device. For example, don't use the pressure washer to whiten your teeth or power wash your grand-babies. This is probably the most detailed section in the user's guide.

4. **Troubleshooting.** This section describes how to fix your pressure washer if it isn't working. It is specifically for men who, on an assembly scale of 1 to 10, are actually a 3. If your own method of assembly isn't working, this section will help you redo it.

Locate your Bible. Find and underline 2 Timothy 3:16—17:

All Scripture is inspired by God and profitable for teaching, for reproof, for correction, for training in righteousness; so that the man of God may be adequate, equipped for every good work.

The Bible is the owner's manual for Christian living. Like the owner's manual for the pressure washer, God's Word also has four general categories of instruction spread throughout all sixty-six books:

1. **Design.** The Bible was designed and "breathed out by God." God's Word convinces us that, behind the Bible, there

is "intelligent design." Men didn't just decide to write it one afternoon. No, it was "breathed out" through the pens of writers over the course of centuries past.

2. **Purpose.** The Bible has a very specific purpose—to teach men and women God's ways and train them in righteous living. The Bible is for sinners to know God, understand His holiness, appreciate God's love for them, worship Him, love His Son Jesus, be saved through His substitutionary sacrifice on the cross, and be changed into Christ-followers.

3. **Warnings.** The Bible gives many warnings and serves to correct and rebuke ungodly living, attitudes, and emotions. Even more than that, it warns about the consequences of rejecting its teachings. It warns about ignoring God's instructions and rejecting His Son Jesus for salvation.

4. **Troubleshooting.** The Bible also has "troubleshooting" instructions for when life gets real bumpy and hardships bring discouragement and despair. It teaches us how to be "complete, equipped for every good work" even when the bottom falls out of our expectations.

Throughout my many years of counseling, it's been my experience that people who want real, long-term help benefit greatly from understanding biblical principles.

That's where I fit in as a counselor—trying to help them understand those biblical principles. While the Bible doesn't directly deal with difficult sons- and daughters-in-law, it does offer great insight into conflict resolution, Christian character development, and preserving "unity and the bond of peace" in God's family.

This book is about what can be one of life's most difficult relationships, the relationship between a father and mother and their son- or daughter-in-law. The biblical owner's manual, therefore, is extremely important in guiding many families through the quagmire of these relationships. Remember, not every son- or daughter-in-law is toxic or extremely difficult. Many are delightful people and a blessing to the families they join. The focus of this book, however, is about those sons- or daughters-in-law who are very difficult to have a relationship with and who create havoc in fine Christian families.

CHAPTER THREE

The Transfer of Power

The 2016 political contest between presidential candidates Hillary Clinton (the established candidate, the Insider) and Donald Trump (the Outsider) was very interesting, to say the least. The candidates battled fiercely, chopping away at each other and their predecessor, President Obama. Obama had served in office for nearly eight years, doing exactly what he thought was in the best interest of the good old USA. Thinking and hoping that the new president would be Hillary Clinton, Obama was confident his legacy would last and the transfer of power would be a rather simple matter. It didn't turn out as he'd hoped.

After Trump's stunning victory, President Obama and President-Elect Trump met in what was a superficial yet peaceful meeting, filled with accolades and promised cooperation. The transfer of power began to unfold. However, over the next couple of months, cooperation waned, disagreements increased, tension grew, and the transfer of power became very bumpy. The "insiders" weren't cooperative and the "outsider" was determined to displace a lot of the insider's previous plans and objectives.

Obama wanted to preserve his legacy, but Trump had his own agenda. He promised that after his inauguration in January 2017, things were going to be quite different. He was determined to discard many, if not all, of Obama's executive orders, cancel what he deemed to be ineffective programs, and initiate his own agenda as quickly as possible. As in so many cases, ego got in the way of a successful and smooth transfer of power. As of January 2017, it seemed Obama and Trump couldn't agree on anything. One thing was for certain: whether you liked it or not, a new sheriff was in town!

Within this unprecedented presidential election saga, I see an illustration of what takes place in family life when a son or daughter falls in love with an "outsider."

Parents have a responsibility to do what is in the best interest of their children. They want their children to be happy and secure, to become independent, well-functioning members of society. They commit their lives to this pursuit and put in a lot of time, energy, and effort.

So when your child packs his belongings into a dilapidated Ford pickup and heads off to college, his first job or apartment, you watch with thanksgiving in your heart because you've achieved your goal. You're so proud and rightfully so. You gave your child the tools, the resources, and the freedom to be independent, make his or her own decisions, and suffer the consequences whatever they might be.

However, when your child meets, dates, "falls in love" with, and brings home Mr. or Miss Outsider to meet you, declaring they want to marry, it can be a major concern for parents. Mr. or Miss Outsider might initially seem like a very normal person. However, it doesn't really make any difference what kind of person the outsider seems to be because, the truth is, adding any kind of son- or daughter-in-law to the family unit is risky business. This Mr. or Miss Outsider is a new threat to their family unit—a stranger who is suddenly right in the middle of their family life, whether the parents like it or not. This outsider begins to challenge their son or daughter with different opinions and ideas, and to influence their child's decision making. And just like that, the "transfer of power," or realignment of parental responsibilities, is underway. It may be bumpy, but it's underway regardless.

With all of the effort, time, and energy put into raising their child, it's more than understandable for parents to experience feelings of frustration and fear when this happens. Almost every parent experiences a kind of separation anxiety when their son or daughter gets into a serious dating or courting relationship. It won't be long until their son or daughter wants to spend more time with their dating partner than around the kitchen table playing UNO with them. Their son or daughter likes spending time with their dating partner's parents and siblings as well. They might even try each other's churches. Changes are starting to develop in their son or daughter as affections are realigning and transition begins. Your other children also feel the changes in the relationship with their sibling. Sometimes, feelings of jealousy, dislike, intimidation, insecurity, and frustration become very evident. Everyone in the family can experience major adjustments as a new dating relationship begins to transition into something totally different. It's a scary time, I know. As I write, I can almost feel the insecurity developing in Dad and Mom. It's hard to know what to do.

When this happens, many parents begin an assessment of the outsider. Is he or she good enough for my child? Is he or she spiritually minded, financially stable, career oriented, responsible, and/or emotionally healthy? It's not long before parents begin to bring up topics like spiritual beliefs, dating etiquette, curfews, and physical touching. But they are often met with disagreement or disapproval. Their child is in a "high speed" relationship, and Dad and Mom are still in "first gear" trying desperately to keep up.

Fearful about whether or not their legacy of family tradition, beliefs, and customs will stand, some parents begin to push back against the challenge of new opinions and new values from the outsider. After all, most parents are aware of the serious nature of the marital commitment the newly married "love birds" will eventually face. They're just trying to help.

There are two different types of "outsiders." The first is a kind and caring outsider. This person is good-natured, flexible, tolerant, and mature. They are easy to be with and aren't threatened by your family. You will be blessed if your child brings home a kind and caring outsider.

But the second kind is a toxic outsider. Such persons are difficult to be around. You can feel their negative energy almost immediately when they enter the room. They are very self-centered, self-willed, self-righteous, self-justifying, and self-consumed. Trouble is on the horizon if your son or daughter brings home one of these!

There are two different types of "outsiders."
The first is a kind and caring outsider. You will
be blessed if your child brings home a kind
and caring outsider.

When the child gets engaged to a toxic outsider, reality sets in—the outsider can begin dismantling or cutting into your "establishment's" historical accomplishments, values, and traditions. This is the case for many concerned parents. You might even hear a parent say, "I don't like the changes in my son or daughter since he or she started dating so and so." Of course, Dad and Mom would prefer their child marry someone whom they can agree with and believe in, and someone who validates them and supports their traditional values and beliefs—in other words, a kind and caring outsider who is compassionate and understanding of Dad and Mom! This would make the transfer of power so much easier. But this is not always the case.

Of course, once their child is engaged to a toxic outsider, parents are backed into a corner, reluctantly needing to agree on a meaningful "transfer of power" prior to the "inauguration" or wedding, even if it's merely for show. So, in spite of their differences, parents will agree to support and help the engaged couple and go on to help make preparations for the wedding and life afterward. However, some parents just can't get over a toxic outsider taking over their son or daughter while ignoring their counsel, legacy, and traditions. So, they continue to resist, argue, and complain about what has happened. This is how fathers- and mothers-in-law get such a poor reputation—they don't respect this necessary "transition" that is taking place and don't know how to manage the negative energy the toxic outsider brings into their family.

Just as Trump took over the office of president in January 2017, whether the "establishment" liked it or not, your son's or daughter's wedding took place or will take place in the future, whether you like it or not. As a parent in this situation, your job now is to learn how to live with the toxic outsider who has a new agenda with your child (which may or may not include you).

With God's help, I hope this book will help you adjust to these new circumstances you find difficult. Your response to the outsider entering your family unit will have a great deal to do with determining your future happiness or continued relationship with your child. I hope the lessons learned will also help the outsider eventually come to appreciate your previous years of great parenting and be sensitive to your legacy as well.

CHAPTER FOUR

Dealing with the Difficult Outsider

Let's go back to that moment your child brings home Mr. or Miss Outsider. This person your child wants to marry may have a cross tattooed on their neck, a ring the size of a silver dollar in their nostril, and purple hair. Or, he or she could be dressed to perfection, without a wrinkle, be well-shaven, and even somewhat religious. Perhaps their parents are divorced, have addiction issues, live on the other side of the tracks, or they may attend church, be well-off financially, and love fishing. Whatever the differences or similarities are on the surface, Mr. or Miss Outsider is a difficult person who wants the world to orbit around them. And your child announces he or she wants to marry this person. This outsider now wants your child to develop new relationships with his or her family and spend less time with your family. No matter how you slice it, it makes for a tough time.

The person your child is wanting to marry has zero regard for the plus or minus 20 years you've sacrificially parented, loved, cared for, taught, fed, disciplined, and enjoyed your child. This person's only concern is self-oriented, and your relationship with your child has gotten in the way, has become intimidating or threatening, and is unnecessary, according to Mr. or Miss Outsider. The reasons for this are many. It could be that they've had a bumpy home life. Maybe they're not a Christian, or they're just very self-focused, insecure, and immature. You might even feel your future son- or daughter-in-law just doesn't like you (and that might be true). Regardless, this makes for a difficult time for mom and dad.

After the wedding and for years to come, you walk on pins and needles. You listen to continual rants, endure endless criticism, overlook snide remarks, and tolerate the put-downs from your son- or daughter-in-law and maybe even your own child. Your son- or daughter-in-law gradually attempts to sever or marginalize your relationship with your child. He or she may even try to justify and defend their behavior using the following flawed logic:

- To "leave and cleave" justifies his or her sinful behavior.

- To be indifferent or uncaring to their father- or mother-in-law isn't dishonoring parents.

- Abusive treatment by him or her is considered setting "boundaries."

- Tough love means "doing it my way."

None of this unbiblical "logic" makes parents very happy. However, it does demonstrate how sinful sons- or daughters-in-law may attempt to justify or defend their abusive treatment of their fathers- or mothers-in-law. It's troubling to say this, but all four of the above happen every day with difficult sons- or daughters-in-law who are unbelievers or professing Christians who don't understand biblical servanthood, obedience, and application of divine truth.

Dear readers, if you find yourself as the parents in this kind of situation, time is on your side. BUT you must not lose the relationship with your son or daughter along the way by arguing, fighting, offering unwanted opinions, or belittling your son or daughter's spouse. You must learn to do six things:

- **Smile a lot.** Colossians 4:5 says, "Conduct yourselves with wisdom toward outsiders." Your countenance is important.

- **Keep your mouth shut.** See James 3:5–10 on the tongue. "It is a restless evil and full of deadly poison" (verse 8).

- **Persevere in prayer.** Meditate on the exhortation in Philippians 4:6–7. "Be anxious for nothing [not even in the difficulties with a toxic son- or daughter-in-law], but in everything by prayer and supplication with thanksgiving let your requests be made known to God. And the peace of God, which surpasses all comprehension, will guard your hearts and your minds in Christ Jesus." Always remember God is a very present help in the time of need.

- **Be flexible.** Proverbs 3:5–6 commands us to "trust in the Lord with all your heart and do not lean on your own understanding. In all your ways acknowledge him, and he will make straight your paths." Not all situations are for you to manage or control. You must learn to live in the tension of different opinions and behaviors. Remember that, behind the scenes, God is constantly at work in the hearts of everyone involved. So you can trust Him, keep a low profile, and remain flexible.

- **Let the hurtful words and actions slide off you, like water off a duck's back.** Ephesians 4:31 says, "Let all bitterness and wrath and anger … be put away from you, along with all malice."

- **If and when you do speak, do so by "speaking the truth in love" (Ephesians 4:15) and with a healthy dose of kindness and patience.** Remember your words are like bullets; once they are spoken, you can't retrieve them. Colossians 4:6 says, "Let your speech always be with grace … so that you will know how you should respond to each person." So be very careful with your words.

If you find yourself in this situation, I encourage you to focus on preserving the relationship with your child. Follow the above principles and the principles from Scripture in the next chapter as you interact with their difficult spouse. Remember that this is a marathon, not a sprint. Do it for the sake of your child and the love you have for her or him.

CHAPTER FIVE

Foundational Principles

Before we get into the stories about difficult sons- and daughters-in-law, let's lay a biblical foundation for processing what's ahead of us. As the song goes, "Let's start at the very beginning, a very good place to start."

But start at the beginning of what? The starting point for some is different from the starting point for others. Some are just beginning to deal with their child in the dating process, and others are just beginning to deal with their child in a difficult marriage. The dating or marriage race was probably already underway by the time you got this book, so put on your parental sneakers and let's go to work. But don't lose heart because dating, engagement, and eventual marriage to an outsider is a marathon, not a 100-yard dash. You have plenty of time to catch up.

I want to assure you I'm not using the term "outsider" in a negative way but in a way to underscore who is part of your original family unit and who is not. Even your child will be an outsider to his or her spouse's family unit. It goes both ways. There are many biblical passages that speak to the subject of people who fall into the category of an outsider and Jesus' loving response. So let's put some thought into a few foundational principles for good relationships with outsiders.

1. Selfless and sacrificial attitudes and actions lay the foundation for future relationships.

Let me remind you that Gentiles (which we are, if we aren't of Jewish descent) were considered outsiders—people who were "separate from Christ, excluded from the commonwealth of Israel, and strangers to the covenants of promise, having no hope and without God in the world" and those "who formerly were far off [but] have been brought near by the blood of Christ" (Ephesians 2:11–14). What we learn from God's Word is that outsiders are brought into God's family by the selfless and sacrificial work of Christ.

This example helps when dealing with a difficult or toxic son- or daughter-in-law. The quality of your relationship with this outsider will depend on your selfless and sacrificial attitudes and actions displayed over many years. John 3:16 says, "For God so loved . . . ." That same quality of love should be a distinguishing mark of dads and moms who wish to have a long-term, healthy relationship with their son- or daughter-in-law. According to Christ, the mark of true discipleship is that we love others: "By this all men will know that you are My disciples, if you have love for one another" (John 13:35).

2. Courageous, intentional actions are required to develop meaningful relationships.

Consider the Samaritan woman of John 4. The Samaritans were outsiders to the Jews. Generally, Jews had nothing to do with the Samaritans. They were spiritual and social outcasts. This is why the woman at the well asked Jesus, "'How is it that You, being a Jew, ask me [an outsider] for a drink since I am a Samaritan woman?' (For Jews have no dealings with Samaritans)" (John 4:9). Even Jesus' disciples marveled that He was talking to this outsider woman (John 4:27).

It took courage and intentionality for Jesus to interact with this Samaritan outsider. Not only that, He also confronted her sinful lifestyle with grace and compassion. He responded to her with love, even though she had five husbands and was living with another man.

The same is true for us—any kind of meaningful, spiritual progress in relationships with outsiders demands courageous and intentional actions. It takes intentional courage to wade into their difficult and often pain-filled life story. Many outsiders come into a family unit with differing religious beliefs, a lot of personal baggage, hurt from the past, fears of the future, and insecurities today. It will take much intentional courage, strategy, and compassion to suck it up, be a listener, and offer counsel or help when invited to do so.

3. **Religiosity won't communicate love; practical biblical principles heal relationships.**

You all know the story of the Good Samaritan in Luke 10:30–37. A traveling man had a stroke of bad luck, fell among robbers, was beaten, and left half dead. A priest saw him and passed by, and so did a Levite, both religious men leaving the traveler to die. Then appeared another man, a Samaritan. When he saw the injured man, "he felt compassion, and came to him and bandaged up his wounds, pouring oil and wine on them; and he put him on his own beast, and brought him to an inn and took care of him" (Luke 10:33–34). Keep in mind, the injured man was an outsider to the benevolent Samaritan. And the religious priest and Levite, who represent the insiders, wouldn't lift a finger to help this poor soul.

Here's something to think about: religion or religious training will never touch the life of an outsider without compassion and a willingness to be "hands on." We must be willing to move from just religiosity to practical and biblical application in order to demonstrate real Christian compassion and love to the outsider.

4. **Modeling genuine Christian faith and love affects difficult relationships.**

There's an old saying I have taped in my first Bible. It goes like this: "No matter how high you jump or how loud you shout, the thing that really matters is how you walk when you come down." Lifestyle is very important to Jesus, and it should be to us as well. I want to leave you with some Bible verses for your personal meditation. They contain vital counsel you'll need going forward:

> Keep a good conscience so that in the thing in which you are slandered, those [outsiders] who revile your good behavior in Christ will be put to shame. (1 Peter 3:16)

> Keep your behavior excellent among the Gentiles [outsiders], so that in the thing in which they slander you as evildoers, they may because of your good deeds, as they observe them, glorify God. . . . For such is the will of God that by doing right you may silence the ignorance of foolish men. (1 Peter 2:12, 15)

> In all things show yourself to be an example of good deeds, with purity in doctrine, dignified, sound in speech which is beyond reproach, so that the opponent [outsider] will be put to shame, having nothing bad to say about us. (Titus 2:7–8)

Prove yourselves to be blameless and innocent, children of God above reproach in the midst of a crooked and perverse generation [outsiders], among whom you appear as lights in the world. (Philippians 2:15)

All of these verses point to the behavior expected of true Christians. Between maintaining a "good conscience," keeping "your behavior excellent," being an "example of good deeds" and remaining "blameless and innocent," the responsibility of being a Christian father- or mother-in-law and truly acting like one is a rather large challenge. Walking through the minefield cluttered with the expectations, traditions, and goals of the outsider is a pretty daunting task, to say nothing about the insecurity, self-centeredness, or dispositional issues your son- or daughter-in-law may bring into your family.

I've learned that the negative attitudes and actions from either the parents or the toxic son- or daughter-in-law can have a tremendous effect on your married child. And this in turn could negatively affect how you live as a Christian. Without practicing the above biblical counsel, you're headed for some very turbulent water in your relationships with your own child, not to mention the outsider he or she married. Therefore, guard and maintain your Christ-centered testimony before the outsider and your child. Your child expects you to practice what you preach, even if times are difficult.

Part Two
The Role of Protective Resources

CHAPTER
SIX

"My Child, What Are You Doing?"

The Whites are a great example of healthy family life. They serve the Lord together, pray together, play together, and live life together. Being around them, you can feel the love they have for one another as they tease and laugh at each other's jokes. It's a perfect illustration of what families are all about.

But this doesn't mean they haven't had bumps in the road. Several years ago, their oldest son (let's call him Steve) went off to college to study engineering. He was a good student, a committed Christian, and a self-disciplined, hard worker. During his first semester, he met Angie. They started dating, and before you could say, "Jack, be nimble," they were pretty serious.

Dad and Mom naturally wanted to get to know Angie. Since the college was close to their home, Steve brought Angie over for dinner, games, and movies. The Whites were very involved with all of their children's friends, and they often had many teenagers hanging out at their home. The evening

Steve brought Angie over was no different. The Whites' home was busy, and almost everyone jumped into the fun and games as usual. Everything seemed to be going well, except Angie wasn't very social. Steve's mother picked up on this quickly. She noticed some of Angie's facial expressions when Steve was enjoying the company of other guys and gals. Angie seemed threatened by Steve's friendships.

> **What do you think caused Angie's feelings about Steve's friendships? As a parent, would this behavior bother you? If so, how would you handle the situation?**

Over the next few months, Steve and Angie continued to grow close, but Angie wasn't as interested in coming to the family home for fun and games. When Steve was at home without Angie, she would send him an endless number of texts, asking him questions and wanting him to call. And she would pout or sulk if he didn't respond immediately. It seemed like Angie didn't want to share Steve with anyone, not even his parents. Dad and Mom became more concerned.

As they continued to date, Steve started spending more time at Angie's, and they attended church together occasionally. When Mom would try to talk with Angie about spiritual matters, Angie didn't have much spiritual insight and showed little interest in the Bible. This also was a matter of great concern to the whole family. Even Steve's friends questioned Angie's spiritual life.

Over time, it became obvious that Angie wanted Steve all to herself. She was unhappy that Steve was so involved with his family and friends. She wanted him to be with her all the time, and she became sad or angry when he wasn't. Dad and Mom continued to invite Angie over for family dinners, but she would only come occasionally. They treated Angie respectfully, but it wasn't always an easy task. Dad and Mom grew increasingly worried about Steve and the effects this relationship was having on him, his friends, and his family.

To make matters worse, Steve and Angie started having sex. In Steve's heart of hearts, he knew this was wrong, but sexual urges often trump shallow convictions. When Angie needed his attention, she would ask him to lay with her on the bed, and he would give in. And, well, you don't need to be a rocket scientist to figure out why this was a bad idea! This didn't excuse or justify Steve's sin, and he accepted full responsibility. However, that only complicated the situation, because when Steve tried to stop having sex with Angie in obedience to God, Angie took this as evidence that he didn't love her and used her tears to manipulate him! Her blatant lack of spiritual conviction alarmed Steve's Dad and Mom, but what were they to do?

How would you explain Angie's tears to Steve?
How would you handle an adult son or daughter
who's having premarital sex?

Steve's siblings, friends, and other family members also observed that this was not a good situation and noticed how Angie was not a good match for Steve. Steve was beginning to question Angie's motives as well, but he "loved" her, whatever that meant. Several family members and friends had talked privately with Steve about their observations of his and Angie's relationship at various times, but Steve didn't (or couldn't, or wouldn't) listen. Even when he did listen, he would vacillate back and forth and never take action to deal with Angie's manipulative ways.

Eventually, the White family and several of Steve's friends gathered up the courage to sit down with Steve and have a type of intervention. They collectively communicated their concerns about the unhealthy nature of his relationship with Angie. Now it was time for him to decide if he was in or out of the relationship.

Steve struggled with their intervention. He could recognize some of Angie's manipulative ways. But he was either infatuated or in love with Angie and frankly, they had some fun times together. The sexual factor also made decision-making very difficult. Thankfully, Steve broke off his relationship with Angie shortly after that. He soon confessed that he felt great relief, as if a 100-pound sack was taken off his back. This was good news to Steve's family and friends, and I'm glad to say, Steve has never looked back.

> This intervention had good results, but was this
> a good strategy? Why or why not?

Many families can relate to this story and some have actually lived through something very similar. It's a common beginning to the boy-meets-girl saga. When a guy and girl start dating, it's a time of evaluation, exploration, excitement, and high expectations for everyone. It's a time when Dad and Mom want to share in their child's excitement, help them evaluate, and ask lots of probing questions. Let's face it—Mom and Dad have their own extremely high expectations! But this is what the dating phase is all about. It's a time for learning, listening to others, and hopefully, laughing along the way.

In the case of Steve and his parents, the dark clouds of a bad relationship moved in, indicating a storm was brewing. Uncertainty began to set in for everyone—his parents grew anxious, his siblings and friends sensed things weren't right. Thankfully, they communicated this to Steve. The intervention meeting was the sun trying to shine through the storm clouds. Fortunately, Steve saw the light and ended the relationship, avoiding what would have been disastrous for all involved.

Some would say I'm an eternal optimist. It's mostly true, and I do get excited when young people begin dating. However, I'm not naive. Many families have or will experience a situation similar to that of the Whites, but with a very different outcome. Their adult child refuses to be objective, rejects any helpful advice, justifies their relationship and moves forward in a relationship with a toxic person. The consequences are devastating, aren't they? This is the time when protective resources are most needed. If you find yourself in a situation like this, can you think of someone who might be able to speak truth to your adult child? Maybe a coach, neighbor, pastor, mentor, uncle or aunt, or grandparent? How about God? Trust Him with your prayers. He cares about your family.

CHAPTER SEVEN

Protective Resources

I've been a hunter for many, many years. One of my favorite times of year is the fall in Colorado—when the leaves are turning yellow, there's frost on the seat of your four-wheeler, and steam is rising from small creeks and watering holes where deer and elk frequently drink. Taking a walk through the forest on one of those brisk mornings truly restores my soul.

On those brisk autumn mornings, though, there is something else going on behind the scenes. It's the start of the breeding season—or "the rut," as it's called—for both deer and elk. Breeding season starts in the fall and only lasts a brief period of time. The buck deer (males) start getting larger necks and begin the long, hard process of pursuing does (females) and fighting with other bucks that challenge their breeding rights. The same happens with the elk. The bulls (males) begin gathering up a herd of cows (females) for breeding purposes, and at the same time try to defend their breeding rights against intruding bulls by some serious fighting.

During breeding season, both bucks and bulls mysteriously exchange their natural protective senses (i.e., hiding in the timber, feeding only at night, avoiding humans, and staying alert) for unrestrained breeding rights. They get so caught up in the pursuit of does and cows that they become careless and neglect to use their protective resources like ears, eyes, and sense of smell. These senses normally serve as guardrails to protect them throughout the year, and when they disregard them in pursuit of breeding partners, they can fall prey to the danger that lurks in the forest—namely me and thousands of other hunters!

At the risk of being too careless with my comparisons, Steve from our previous story fell into the same kind of danger as the bulls and bucks when he was pursuing Angie. After they met, the red lights or guardrails of wisdom, caution, and concern mysteriously began to dim. Driven by their natural impulses, their dating or courting relationship accelerated into a more physical union. They laid aside their protective resources like God's Word, Steve's parents' concern, and even the counsel of friends. And they put themselves in a very dangerous spot, vulnerable to the Devil who prowls around like a roaring lion, seeking someone to devour (1 Peter 5:8).

When a couple start down the dating path, it's quite easy for them to be taken over by their emotions, leading to self-deception and a lack of discernment. Young people preparing for marriage are especially vulnerable. It's so difficult for them to slow down long enough to take a deep breath, hit the pause button, get their minds off their physical attractions, and face hard dating issues head on. Frankly, sexual appetites and urges can and often will blur a person's view of a relationship.

How would you counsel Steve and Angie about their physical relationship?

It's difficult to keep the proper perspective about a relationship when it is sexually super-charged and running hot. Like a buck deer or a bull elk, a hasty guy or girl infatuated or "in love" with someone will do the craziest things. They think they can ignore the guardrails of their protective resources and recklessly pursue the relationship, only to find themselves stuck in the mud of a very unfortunate relationship later on.

This is precisely why those protective resources—accountability relationships and wise premarital counsel—are crucial. Of course, the Scriptures encourage us to seek help from God (the Mighty Counselor) and counsel from parents, friends, pastors, or other trained counselors. Notice just a few verses on this subject:

A wise man will hear and increase in learning, and a man of understanding will acquire wise counsel. (Proverbs 1:5)

Where there is no guidance the people fall, but in abundance of counselors there is victory. (Proverbs 11:14)

The way of a fool is right in his own eyes, but a wise man is he who listens to counsel. (Proverbs 12:15)

Without consultation, plans are frustrated, but with many counselors they succeed. (Proverbs 15:22)

Listen to counsel and accept discipline, that you may be wise the rest of your days. (Proverbs 19:20)

Think back to Steve and Angie's story. Steve's family and friends played a valuable role in helping him sift through the debris of an unhealthy relationship. In Proverbs 27:17, we're reminded that "iron sharpens iron, so one man sharpens another." As finite individuals, we don't always have all the answers. Accountability relationships protect us and give us a better understanding of dating relationships as well as insights into our personal weaknesses and character deficiencies.

Premarital counseling helps in this area also. There's no greater opportunity to help a young couple make healthy, informed, and sound decisions about marriage than premarital counseling. As the old sayings go, "an ounce of prevention is worth a pound of cure," and "preventative medicine is better than corrective surgery." We will delve into the benefits of premarital counseling in the next chapter.

How would you present the need for premarital counseling to your son or daughter?

Thankfully Steve listened to the counsel of his family and friends. Unfortunately, couples don't always listen to wise counsel. Infatuation looks past character flaws, and lust and denial take precedence over rational thinking. It's very difficult to stop and listen to counsel that threatens your relationship. Failure to address issues like emotional instability, manipulation, undisciplined love, or speedy infatuation often leads both guys and gals into questionable relationships with toxic individuals. These toxic dating partners try to hide negative emotions and unacceptable behaviors in order to avoid being exposed for what and who they really are. They manage their public image well, and can often keep up their disguise until after the wedding. But one telltale sign of a toxic person is their reluctance to take advantage of valuable protective resources like premarital counseling, relationships with accountability, and insight from parents and friends. They cannot tolerate objective or critical voices and usually respond by isolating themselves and their dating partner from family and friends.

Who would you name as your protective resources?

Proverbs 3:21 sums it up pretty well: "My son ... keep sound wisdom and discretion." In other words, be mentally sharp and don't rely on your emotions. "The mind of the prudent acquires knowledge, and the ear of the wise seeks knowledge" (Proverbs 18:15). Emotions alone will lead a person down a very dark and dangerous path. Wisdom applied and knowledge used both come through the Word of God. Godly accountability partners and wise biblical counsel will help build a healthy relationship.

Dating, courtship, or whatever you want to call it, is dangerous territory and is not something to attempt without engaging your protective resources. Don't go it alone! Instead, rely on the insights of others who care about you and have your best interests in mind: your parents, siblings, pastors, friends, even the family pet!

As a parent, do your best to encourage your adult child to use their protective resources. But how do you go about doing that? Well, here are some suggestions:

1. **Know and understand your adult child.** Some adult children are more open to suggestions or guidance than others. It's important to understand how they think and what or whom they would be more likely to listen to. Frankly, it's not always the parents. I see this in my adult children.

Some ask my opinion, while others want to go it alone. To those who want my guidance, I can personally give my opinion, while those who don't seek my advice generally find other accountability sources. Not understanding your adult child can have disappointing consequences. It's not wise to push your opinion on an adult child who isn't interested in your opinion.

2. **Encourage your adult child to find a mentor.** Mentoring relationships are very important to young adults. They look up to other successful spiritual mentors and desire to learn from them. Many personal and deep discussions take place in these relationships. Don't minimize the importance of this to your adult children. They need someone to talk to (other than their parents) who will hold them accountable. In my own experience as a father, my children all benefited from these mentoring-type relationships whether spiritual, professional, or practical.

3. **Set an example of seeking advice and counsel.** Try to teach them that none of us has all the answers to life's questions, and at times all of us must seek wisdom from others. Model this for your adult children by letting them know about of your accountability partners or protective resources that you rely upon in the parenting of adult children. Be humble, be a learner, and seek the advice of others.

———————————————

There's no greater opportunity to help a young couple make healthy, informed, and sound decisions about marriage than premarital counseling.

———————————————

CHAPTER EIGHT

Effective Premarital Counseling

As a rancher, I've learned some important lessons over the years. One of them is this: there's no need to shut the gate after the cows get out. It's essential to shut the gate before the cows escape. The same is true with your son or daughter regarding dating. It's important they become aware of the potential consequences of poor dating choices sooner than later. Be proactive and help your adult child understand this transition even before he or she starts dating.

Let's consider an example from the Bible of some protective counsel. Isaac instructed Jacob in Genesis 28:1: "You shall not take a wife from the daughters of Canaan." I assume the same counsel was given to Esau, Jacob's brother. Esau, however, rejected his father's counsel and chose two wives from among the neighboring Hittite women, and as a result he "brought grief to Isaac and Rebekah [his father and mother]" (Genesis 26:35). Disobedience to his father's premarital counsel brought hardship on the entire family.

What would be your strategy if your adult child began dating a non-Christian?

Take note of Isaac's counsel to his sons. As Christians, we must be careful to instruct our young adults not to marry a person who doesn't belong to the family of God through a personal relationship with Jesus Christ. If your child brings home an unbeliever, you will be on very touchy footing in your family relationships, just like Isaac and Rebekah with Esau and his wives. Furthermore, dating anybody with severe emotional issues like depression, negativity, severe anger, or insecurities can lead to a minefield for any family to navigate. Your adult child needs to be warned about these dangerous relationships long before he or she starts dating. Waiting to give advice until your child starts dating is like shutting the gate after the cows get out.

Chances are certainly better for long-term family fellowship if your adult child brings home a God-fearing, well-balanced son-in-law or daughter-in-law like Ruth (see Ruth 1:16–17), who puts into motion biblical principles for living and actually blends nicely into your family. The addition of such an outsider is a real blessing to any family.

Many churches encourage and are committed to pre-engagement and premarital counseling as a necessary prerequisite before performing a wedding. This is a good thing, and more churches should be intentional about premarital counseling. But what makes up a good premarital counseling program? Let's look at a few key components:

1. Premarital counseling should be based on biblical content. Most premarital counseling programs cover subjects like communication, the roles of husband and wife, finances, and sex. These are all extremely important topics to cover. Occasionally there is discussion about children, employment, marital expectations, church life, and even parenting goals. These are all terrific segments of a meaningful premarital program. Using the Bible as a reference gives God's instruction about how each segment is lived out. Very important! However, the spiritual life of both parties is a subject often overlooked. Are they both Christians or not? Are they committed to biblical teaching, and do they apply biblical disciplines to their relationship? Do they demonstrate spiritual growth? Do they have shared ministry objectives?

Personally, I would also add a discussion about relationships with each other's parents. What does it mean to leave one's father and mother and cleave to one's spouse (Genesis 2:24)? What expectations do the guy and gal have about their relationships with parents and in-laws as they establish their own family unit? What are ways they can seek to honor their future father- and mother-in-law (Ephesians 6:2)?

2. Premarital counseling should explore compatibility issues.

Some premarital counseling programs also include personality testing. The Taylor-Johnson Temperament Analysis, the Myers-Briggs Type Indicator assessment, and the Prepare/Enrich relationship assessment are just a few that are available. I find these profiles very helpful for understanding marital compatibility as well as exposing personality traits that can be potentially abusive, controlling, divisive, or destructive. Couples need to understand as much as possible about any personality disorders or emotional imbalance before they get married. These personality assessments can indicate extreme insecurity, hostility, indifference, lack of sensitivity, or compulsive behavior. Should that be the case, dating partner, spouse and in-laws, BEWARE!!! Premarital counseling is also a time to help a couple learn how to deal correctly with compatibility differences. These tests can also be very encouraging to a couple because they show relational strengths, not just weaknesses. This is a good thing. I see the test as a positive tool that build awareness and introduces some reality into the relationship.

During my years of premarital work, I've been very clear with some couples that they shouldn't marry for obvious reasons, or that they should give their premarital relationship more time. I've even brought their parents into my office to explain my position. But often it's like talking to a rock or a brick wall. Looking back now, far too many of those couples are either divorced or in deep marital trouble Furthermore, many of their extended families have been broken apart by a difficult son- or daughter-in-law.

3. Premarital counseling should also expose personal and relational weaknesses.

In his book titled *How to Avoid Marrying a Jerk*, John Van Epp explains what he calls RAM (Relationship Attachment Model).[1] One of the greatest deterrents to marrying a jerk involves keeping five critical elements in balance. They are knowledge, trust, reliance, commitment, and intimacy. Allow me to explain in my own words.

Ideally, relationships begin with knowledge about the person you're dating. As your knowledge of a person grows, you can be more trusting of that person. But the amount of trust should never exceed what knowledge allows. The same is true of relying on a person. You shouldn't rely on a person more than your knowledge of them allows. A wise person wouldn't commit to a person unless their knowledge supports it. And finally, becoming intimate physically without considering biblical and personal knowledge is beyond foolish.

In other words, keep knowledge as the primary guardrail to protect you from unwise emotions that can lead to premature trust, reliance, commitment, or foolish and unbiblical intimacy. You run the risk of marrying a jerk if any of the other four elements takes precedence over the

[1] John Van Epp, *How to Avoid Marrying a Jerk* (McGraw-Hill, 2007), 22–25.

knowledge of your dating partner. Don't trust, don't rely, don't commit, and don't become intimate with a person you don't know and know well.

The goal of dating is to grow your knowledge of the person. So, if you are in such a relationship, take mental notes, and don't ignore obvious weaknesses, immaturity, and personality defects like anger, impatience, and self-centered behaviors and attitudes in the person you're dating. Don't be a fool and think that marriage is a fix-all and that with time all will be well. Don't let denial, a desire to be loved, a need for companionship, or peer pressure cause you to compromise or ignore what knowledge tells you about the person you're dating.

A good premarital or pre-engagement counseling program should expose how well or how poorly you know the other person. It also provides a safe environment to discuss some important areas where you need to know more about what the other person thinks, before you can determine whether or not they are worthy of more trust, reliance, commitment, and intimacy.

What happens if intimacy is the goal of dating rather than knowledge?

Having done engagement and premarital counseling for many years, I understand the tremendous role premarital counseling can play in curbing the escalating divorce rates, preventing perpetual unhappiness in marriage, and avoiding the nightmare of a toxic son- or daughter-in-law. Premarital counseling is the one time before marriage that a couple can get an objective opinion about their dating from someone outside their relationship. A third party's godly perspective can expose self-deception or blind spots that don't necessarily show up in the dating process.

Exposing these weaknesses doesn't necessarily mean the couple will always listen, because that isn't the case. As the Bible says, "A scoffer does not love one who reproves him, he will not go to the wise." (Proverbs 15:12) Thankfully, pastors, counselors, and parents are not responsible for outcomes because God is sovereign. But we are responsible to ensure a helpful process is in place and protective resources are available to protect young couples and extended family members from toxic personalities.

If you are a parent whose child is in a dating relationship, start talking now about the necessity of premarital counseling. It doesn't hurt to discuss these things before your child even starts dating. Chances are, your adult child will do some serious dating, so keep premarital counseling on the front burner. If your adult child is already in one of these toxic relationships whether dating or married, help is on the way, so please read on.

CHAPTER
NINE

Where Trouble Begins

In the previous chapter, I briefly mentioned that premarital counseling is a good time for a discussion about relationships with the parents-in-law.

Not long ago, I was doing premarital counseling with a wonderful young couple. Many things were going so well in their relationship. They were growing spiritually together, reading the Bible together, attending a church faithfully, and involved in ministry to others. We had a great time talking about how God was building His life into theirs through their Bible reading and service to others.

As is my custom, I had them do a personality evaluation. When we went over their results, I noticed some interesting differences in their personality types. Jim was more of a logical thinker, so information first passed through his brain, slowly making its way to his heart/feelings. He also showed signs of being abrasive and controlling which, if not addressed, would certainly become problematic in the future. Betty, on the other hand, was more of an emotional feeler. Information passed through her heart/feelings first, gradually making its way to her head. She also seemed a bit reluctant to challenge or confront Jim when there was a disagreement.

In your circle of friends or in your family, can you identify a couple like Jim and Betty?

Later in our counseling, the subject of Betty's parents surfaced, and I quickly found that serious trouble, like a snake, was waiting in the weeds. Betty was under pressure from her parents regarding wedding plans. Her parents felt that they should have a more significant say in the wedding plans since they were paying for much of it. I certainly can understand their logic, but the pressure was beginning to cause trouble for sensitive Betty, and no-nonsense Jim was getting frustrated. Being a cut-and-dry kind of guy, he wanted Betty to do whatever she wanted because it's her wedding, not her parents'. Jim didn't like her parents' interference and was putting his foot down on some of their wedding suggestions. But this only added to Betty's stress because she didn't want to hurt her parents either. The distance between Jim and Betty was widening tangibly. Poor Betty was caught in the middle between Jim and her parents.

This young couple was on the verge of the happiest moments of their lives, with so much promise and everything seemingly going their way. But deep down in the weeds, so much danger, hurt, and unhappiness were waiting like a snake ready to strike. Why? Because a generous dad and mom were on one side of the wedding equation, and a hard-headed future son-in-law was on the other. I could feel the tension building between Jim and Betty, and between Jim and Betty's parents. If Dad and Mom didn't lighten up, and if Jim couldn't understand and respond to Betty's love for her parents, their future relationships would be in serious danger.

I offered to meet with Betty's parents to try to help them understand the situation. It would only be a matter of time before someone would step into the weeds and the snake would strike using hateful words, angry insults, and hurtful actions. Could I diffuse the situation and stop the poison from being injected? Maybe, and there certainly were things Jim, Betty, and Betty's parents could do. Let's look at this from their perspectives and what I might suggest as strategy with each one.

Jim: He needs to understand the potential dangers his black-and-white personality might bring to his and Betty's relationship with her parents. Betty's parents already feel Jim is too controlling in general and that the wedding plan is just another example of his control. I needed to remind Jim of his responsibility to be a servant leader to his wife, and to preserve Betty's relationship with her parents, even if it meant great personal cost. Because Jim is called to love Betty sacrificially (Ephesians 5:25) and to love her as he loves himself (Ephesians 5:33), he must honor her parents and not be critical of them. Betty's relationship with her parents is very important to her, and Jim must be humble and respectful of their involvement, even if he disagrees.

Jim must face conflicts with his future in-laws with patience and Christlike love as the Bible teaches. In fact, he may need to keep his thoughts to himself, step back, and allow Betty to handle communication with them. But more importantly, he needs to be careful not to respond in a childish way or send Betty on a guilt trip for loving her parents. He should remember Proverbs 15:1, "A gentle answer turns away wrath, but a harsh word stirs up anger." Turning the other cheek (Matthew 5:39) as Jesus taught will be an important principle to remember. His job is to display Christlike love and stay out of the weeds.

How would you approach Jim if you were Betty?

Betty: She needs to be careful as well. I reminded her there will be changes to her relationship with her parents. She will feel this struggle, and so will her parents. Patience with her parents is important, but so is honesty concerning their involvement. This is her responsibility, not Jim's. She must help her parents understand that she and Jim are making decisions together. She must defend Jim in response to her

Dad and Mom's criticism. That's one way Betty will respect or reverence Jim (Ephesians 5:33).

Betty must also remember that she is to be a helper to Jim (Genesis 2:18). Being his helper means encouraging Jim not to act in a hateful or indifferent way to her parents. He must learn not to minimize or intimidate her because of her love and care for her parents. Sometimes a husband can become threatening, behave very childishly, and be manipulative to his father- and mother-in-law. This is biblically unacceptable.

It's always important to bear in mind the clear teaching of Ephesians 5:21, which reminds everyone to submit to one another. Practically speaking, it would be a good thing spiritually for Jim and Betty to respond to her parents' expectations with humility and submission, demonstrating the selfless servanthood of Jesus Christ who came "not to be served but to serve." If Jim and Betty desire a loving relationship with Betty's parents, taking the "high road" will protect them from the snake in the weeds.

How would you approach Betty's parents if you were Betty?

Betty's parents: I've been involved in family disputes for decades. When it's all said and done, the best advice I can give to parents and fathers- and mothers-in-law is this: learn to smile a lot, keep your mouth shut and pray. It's basically that simple if you want to have a thriving relationship with your adult child and their extended family. If you want to enjoy your grandchildren, smile, keep your mouth shut and pray. If you want to have happy holidays and pleasant vacations together, smile, keep your mouth shut and pray. If your child or son- or daughter-in-law wants your opinion, they'll ask. Opinions should be invited, not pushed or forced. If your child and their spouse want a messy yard, a trashed garage, or children without shoes playing in the snow, smile, keep your mouth shut and pray.

Using the technique of FOG (Fear-Obligation-Guilt) will not work with your extended family. It will only create emotional distance. There will be opportunities where you can offer assistance or counsel upon request, but to instigate those conversations is rather dangerous. When you plan holiday get-togethers or birthdays, try to eliminate any guilt by closing the conversation with "this is totally up to you and if you are unable to come we understand." Try to eradicate FOG from your relationships, and life will be a whole lot easier. Maybe giving Jim and Betty a budget for the wedding would be better than supervising every aspect of wedding expenses. Let them spend the budgeted money as they see fit. Mom and Dad's job is to do everything they can to stay out of the weeds.

What are some other situations where parents or in-laws need to be careful to avoid FOG?

In conclusion, Jim and Betty responded well to my counsel. Jim realized his lack of understanding for Betty's feelings was driving a wedge between them and her parents. His stubborn opinions created a difficult environment for relationships to thrive. Betty, on the other hand, understood the need to be more assertive with her parents in order to protect Jim's concerns. In spite of some tears and frustrations, our counseling session with Jim and Betty ended on good terms with new, realistic expectations.

CHAPTER TEN

Communicating Disapproval

Because of the nature of my ministry to families, I hear from countless parents who disagree with their son or daughter as to whom they intend to marry. Often a daughter will drag home a guy who doesn't meet the expectations of her parents (don't like his purple Mohawk and earrings). The same is true when it comes to a son bringing home a young lady his parents think is unacceptable (don't like her leather dress, combat boots, and nose ring). These situations raise great concern for parents who've devoted their lives to parenting and preparing their child to marry "Mr. or Miss Perfect." Ideally, parents would always agree with their child, but that's not very realistic. This is precisely why "arranged marriages" are still practiced in some cultures and religions.

Most of us in Western cultures don't accept the "arranged marriage" model for spousal selection. It might seem wiser for parents to pick their son's or daughter's marriage partner, but that's not necessarily acceptable to the young person who must marry someone they don't know.

Since an arranged marriage is probably out of the question, many parents are left wondering, "What should I do if I don't approve of the person my child has chosen to marry?" I've observed three different responses from parents caught in this dilemma:

- **Withdraw:** Some parents choose not to get involved in who their child marries and totally withdraw from giving advice. This is generally the approach of a parent who has become fairly disconnected from their child. They don't really care, or are frightened by the possibility of in-depth conversation, and don't know how to handle the tension.

- **Demand:** On the other extreme, there are parents who impose their opinions, expectations, and demands upon their child, destroying relationships. They continue to be "helicopter parents" of even adult children, managing every detail of their child's being. I've even encountered parents who have excommunicated and shunned their child for proceeding in a relationship they didn't approve of. Of course, these parents represent a radical fringe of either manipulating control freaks or ultra-conservative religious groups, including certain cults and Christian extremists. This would not be the norm for most parents.

• **Caution:** Then there are parents who are concerned and want to learn about the person their child wants to marry. These parents are committed to guiding, teaching, and cautioning their child in productive ways. They are also committed to not controlling or manipulating their child's life, especially when the child is old enough to be responsible for his or her own choices. Nevertheless, these parents can find themselves deeply concerned about their child's choice of a spouse. Their concerns may stem from any number of issues: the potential spouse's irresponsibility or laziness, anger issues, controlling, manipulative, abusive personality, family history, lack of spiritual growth, extreme religious views, or an outright absence of any Christian faith . . . and the list goes on and on.

How do you learn about your child's future spouse without being overly protective and appearing suspicious?

So how do Dad and Mom (future father- and mother-in-law) handle these difficult dating or engagement relationships (see the options above—withdraw, demand, or caution) when concern arises? Honestly, I'm in camp #3 (caution) and would choose to fulfill my responsibility carefully and gently, knowing my relationship with both my child and future son- or daughter-in-law is at stake. Here are some words of caution to consider before carelessly diving head first into your adult child's love relationship:

1. **Whatever you say to your child about your future son-
   or daughter-in-law will eventually get back to your future
   son- or daughter-in-law.** So be very careful how you
   communicate any doubts, caution, or criticism. I just
   recently heard a father refer to his son's new girlfriend
   as a slut. Of course, this got back to her. What do you think
   their relationship will be like if the young couple gets married?
   Do you think she'll ever forget what her future father-in-
   law said about her? I seriously doubt it. It may seem like the
   person your child is dating has a hidden intuition that knows
   the difference between what your child says and what you say
   through your child. Watch what you say.

2. **The emotion between the two love birds can be more
   intense than your child's feelings for you.** This doesn't
   mean your adult child doesn't love you or care about you.
   It just means the child is in love, and that's a pretty powerful
   thing. If a parent carelessly tries to fracture that love, it will
   come with extreme consequences. Dating creates transition,
   and transition can produce insecurity. Insecurity can cause
   unintended responses toward those involved. Be careful.

3. **Pushing back against a growing relationship often ends
   up pushing the two people closer together.** Allowing for
   personal decision making on the part of your adult child
   is far better. Of course, this takes a lot of patience and
   a heart to understand along the way. Pushing a young man

to break up with his girlfriend is like pushing a rope uphill. It's better if your adult child breaks up with a boyfriend or girlfriend on his or her own terms, without parents' threats, demands, conditions, etc. A parent's job is to prepare their adult child to make wise choices and to live life skillfully with discernment and with a reverence for God. Should the adult child refuse the carefully articulated counsel from his or her parents and move forward with an unhealthy relationship, the responsibility belongs to the adult child. Who's to say that in the providence of God, this isn't in His divine plan for your adult child? One of the most difficult spiritual truths to apply in a parent's life is to trust God with their child's decision making. Be patient.

4. **Your adult child will quickly tire of hearing criticism or negative comments about their boyfriend or girlfriend.** You might try communicating your concerns through questions or by sharing your opinion when invited, but then let it rest and trust the Lord. If you continue to nag, it will hurt your relationship with your adult child and with your future son- or daughter-in-law, because it will eventually get back to them. It's better if your concerns come from an outside source—another friend, pastor, or even a book. So often information is better received from someone other than parents. Be instructive rather than a nag.

5. **Everyone's future is at risk.** You need to tread carefully and watch how you communicate. If you make a big deal out of the situation or aren't careful about how you communicate, you can ruin any chance of a good relationship with your future son- or daughter-in-law. They will never understand why you put up such a fuss over your adult child's marriage to them. They'll be convinced you don't like them, disapprove of them, and don't trust them. I've seen very few sons- or daughters-in-law get past those hurt feelings and seek to rebuild relationships. They may tolerate their father- or mother-in-law, but deep down inside they feel unaccepted and criticized. Trust also has been broken between the father and mother and future son- or daughter-in-law because they talked behind their back.

The early stages of your relationship with a future son- or daughter-in-law can be very difficult to navigate. It's important to tread lightly. I recommend that you go back to Chapter 4 and reexamine the six suggestions I gave to minimize the collateral damage that can happen when parents are too negative and or talk too much about a future son- or daughter-in-law. Remember, the goal is to hold on to the long-term relationship with your son or daughter. If you have concerns, express them in careful, loving dialog with your child. But, as I've already said, you must tread lightly! Don't give your future son- or daughter-in-law verbal ammunition to use against you to undermine your relationship with your son or daughter.

I'll close this chapter with one final thought. Remember, confronting your married son or daughter and son- or daughter-in-law is dangerous territory and I'll tell you why. Hurtful or contentious words may be forgiven at best but are never forgotten. Even professing Christians who strongly believe in the principle of forgiveness, find it very difficult to move forward in a relationship after hurtful words are spoken. Your offended or hurt son- or daughter-in-law may offer forgiveness but deep down inside "the way you really feel about me" is permanently etched on your son- or daughter-in-law's mind and heart. Those feelings make relationship restoration and family fellowship very difficult long-term.

Part Three
Recipe For Disaster

CHAPTER ELEVEN

When Disaster Strikes

Imagine taking a nice walk down to the barn to feed the cows, only to be greeted by a nasty rattlesnake. What was going to be a pleasurable morning doing chores quickly turns into a possible disaster and a frightening game of hide-and-seek. You wonder if and how you can go about your business while avoiding the snake, or if you should just shoot the snake and be done with it.

Dealing with a difficult son- or daughter-in-law can be a lot like dealing with that rattlesnake. The outcome can be disastrous. Since we can't get rid of our son- or daughter-in-law, we need to learn how to live with them and not be affected by their harmful and sometimes disastrous bite.

I know some of you won't be able to relate to these feelings because your son- or daughter-in-law is well-balanced, understanding, selfless, and non-threatening. That's a good thing. However, more and more young people are confused, alienated, angry, and very self-focused due to the epidemic narcissism in American homes, which leads to broken and dysfunctional family life. Some don't understand what a good family actually looks like, nor do they realize the impact that a dysfunctional family has had on them. In fact, many are permanently scarred emotionally and ill-equipped to grow a healthy marriage, let alone to form healthy extended family relationships.

When some of these damaged young people find their way into the church and are saved, we praise God and delight in these new converts. However, even as Christians, these young people will have a large amount of baggage that needs to be dealt with. And that baggage doesn't always get dealt with easily or quickly. Therefore, when one of them meets and eventually marries your well-adjusted, innocent child, things can get pretty dicey—especially for you, the unsuspecting father- and mother-in-law.

Navigating through the complicated minefield of anger, insecurity, bitterness, or unrealized expectations that follows can be very challenging. Like with the rattlesnake, disaster can strike when you least expect it. It's very difficult to avoid your son- or daughter-in-law's poisonous bite.

In order to get a better understanding of this subject, I'm submitting the reflections of a young man who has suffered this very thing. It's not just a story about an ugly, failed marriage; more specifically, it's about a very difficult daughter-in-law. It's an all-too-familiar narrative: a Christian family's son marries a professing Christian lady, but then disaster strikes and everyone's world falls apart. As you read, think about the questions I've inserted. They are designed to help you engage more with the story.

I'm Joseph, and I married Susan back in 2009.[1] We met at a Christian college in Kansas. We were friends, but there was no romantic interest. A couple years after graduation, I started thinking about Susan. A couple of my classmates had already gotten married, and I remembered Susan was a lot of fun and pretty smart. What did I have to lose? I gave her a call.

That phone call turned into a renewed friendship, and before we knew it, Susan and I were in a fast-paced dating relationship. After two months, she took a job out of town, putting us in a frustrating, long-distance relationship, and making marriage seem like a more realistic solution. (I look back now and realize I was passionately stupid instead of realistic.) The facts that Susan came from a broken home, had an abusive father, and had just gotten out of a bad relationship with a previous boyfriend were not important to me. Instead, I convinced myself that she really needed me, that God was in our relationship, and that He could easily fix her. (Now I understand that kind of thinking was "misdirected romantic deception.") In a very short time Susan and I were married.

---

[1] I've altered the names and some of the details to protect the contributor's identity.

How can you slow down a "high speed" relationship?

A couple years into our marriage Susan told me, "I don't trust you and I don't respect you." I hadn't thought our marriage was really that bad, but evidently negative emotions had been building within Susan. She was becoming more angry and unable to cope with me or our children. Looking back now, I can see that Susan's problems had more to do with her than our marriage. But our marriage became the demon or the whipping post she blamed for her inner turbulence and hateful outbursts. This marked the beginning of walking on eggshells, trying to stay out of the way, trying to parent our children, and searching for help.

When should Joseph have pursued help?

Since we were both professing Christians, we decided to get involved in ministry together and took on some short-term mission work, thinking it would ease the tension at home. But even that didn't stop the downhill trajectory of our relationship. Looking back, I sacrificed my role as a loving leader in our home in order to keep peace . . . and that was a big mistake! But confrontation was painful and risky at best. Susan had a very dark and dangerous side. It was easier to simply give in, stay out of trouble and have peace at any price.

Susan was quick to find fault with everyone including our pastor, other church leaders, store clerks, other drivers, and even our dearest friends. And she communicated that through critical, rude, and even hateful comments. Forgiveness, understanding, and compassion were never an option because it was always the other person's fault.

What other options did Joseph have?

For example, one day we had a family party at our house, and Susan wanted a few items from the grocery store. I left immediately but returned with something a bit different than what Susan wanted. She started yelling at me right in front of my entire family. As if that wasn't enough, while I was gone she had argued with my sister about how to fix a sandwich! Her behavior spoiled the entire day and was so embarrassing to everyone. I regret my non-action that day. I should have apologized to family members and asked them to leave. Afterward, I could have privately tried to help Susan understand how biblically unacceptable her behavior was. As her husband, doing this was my responsibility, and it would have demonstrated biblical love for her. Instead, I was a coward and did nothing.

Sadly, I'm trapped inside the revolving door of Susan's anger and self-righteous attitudes. And I'm not the only one; my parents and siblings are also stuck in the same revolving door. They can't do anything right as far as Susan is concerned.

My parents are great people, and so many people love them. Yet I have so many painful memories of my wife (their daughter-in-law) lashing out at them, being rude, inconsiderate, and out of control. I am stuck in the middle, forced to choose between Susan, my parents, and siblings. Anytime I try to discuss her childish, inappropriate behavior, Susan explodes, personalizing whatever I've said, and accusing me of siding with my family and not loving her. It would be less painful and more productive if I rammed a pencil up my nose.

How could Joseph's parents help Susan and avoid conflict?

For our children's sake, divorce is not an option. That means I'm stuck married to a very difficult woman. My parents aren't pushy and continue to cautiously reach out to Susan. I constantly make excuses for her bad behavior. At the same time, I hypocritically agree with Susan when she criticizes my parents, simply to cool her down. She has created tremendous division in my relationship with Dad and Mom. I try to not speak poorly of Susan to them. But they're neither blind nor deaf! They know exactly what's going on.

Should "cooling Susan down" be Joseph's only concern?

I don't know what triggers Susan's negative behavior toward my family. It seems they bring out the worst in her.

Could her lack of respect for me carry over to them? Is she jealous of my family and insecure around them? Does her dysfunctional family history drive her to resist being close to my family?

I don't know how to handle such extreme behavior. How do you approach a person who thinks they're never wrong, transfers blame to others, and justifies their inappropriate actions and attitudes? I still feel God wanted me to marry her, but coping on a daily basis is virtually impossible. I admit that I've failed Susan in many ways, especially by not confronting her negative attitudes and ill treatment of others early on regardless of her reactions. That is what I should have done as the God-ordained servant leader of our home.

I know the Lord can enable me to be patient, forgiving, and forbearing with any grievances in our marriage. Thanks for your interest in my situation. — Joseph

---

When disaster strikes like this, it shocks everyone. These kinds of family trials are some of the most painful events a father and mother could ever endure. Maybe you can relate to the mess Joseph and his family face every day. If so, you're not alone. I encourage you to find comfort in the Lord whose "mercies are new every day," and read on.

We will look more carefully at Joseph's story, but first let me encourage parents with these words from James 1:2—4, 12:

Consider it all joy, my brethren when you encounter various trials, knowing that the testing of your faith produces endurance. And let endurance have its perfect result, so that you may be perfect and complete, lacking in nothing. … Blessed is a man who perseveres under trial; for once he has been approved, he will receive the crown of life which the Lord has promised to those who love Him.

These verses give us very relevant instructions and guidance. First, we see that our attitude plays a very important role in dealing with a difficult son- or daughter-in-law. We are to "consider it all joy." In other words, we are to make a conscious effort to face our trial with joy. It's good to know that we have a Great Big God who is "large and in charge."

Second, know that these trials are a testing of your faith. A trial is anything that interrupts our peace, comfort, joy, or happiness. In other words, God wants to test, prove, and increase the quality of your faith. Spiritual maturity is a high priority on God's list.

Finally, we're reminded that trials produce in us endurance, maturity, and perseverance. So, in conclusion, looking at our difficult son- or daughter-in-law through our spiritual eyes will prepare our hearts to act with kindness and to experience true joyfulness even when disaster strikes.

CHAPTER TWELVE

Disaster Disarmed

If you were a rancher like me, you'd appreciate the services of a top-notch cow dog, especially when you run cattle on hundreds of acres covered in oak brush. Cows are pretty smart (and ornery), and they know when you're coming to move them to another pasture or bring them home for the winter. The minute they see you riding close to them on horseback, they take off into the oak brush and hide where you can't reach them by horse or 4-wheeler. It can get pretty frustrating unless you have a good cow dog.

I've had several good cow dogs and a few that weren't worth a nickel. The difference between a good cow dog and a bad one is obedience. If the dog doesn't follow instructions, it causes more problems than it solves. But if the dog is obedient, it will go into the oak brush and drive the cattle out, even if it gets cuts and bruises in the process. And that little obedient dog saves the old cowboy a massive headache while rounding up the cattle.

Let's keep the value of obedience in mind as we unpack Joseph and Susan's story, because obedience disarms disaster. Both Joseph and Susan professed faith in Jesus Christ as Savior and even volunteered for short-term mission experiences. They probably also prayed over meals, carried their Bibles to church, and enrolled their children in Sunday School. They might have even had personal devotions each day. However, something was really missing in the expression of their faith. One critical component was conspicuously absent in their marriage and in their relationship with Joseph's father and mother: the lack of biblical obedience in their lives.

There are many people like Joseph and Susan who are religious and even have an interest in the religious community and service to others. However, their interest is similar to that of a nonreligious person's interest in the local YMCA or health club. It's really more of a social connection than a life-changing, Holy Spirit-empowered life of scriptural obedience.

Why do you think obedience to God's Word is so difficult?

What's missing in Joseph and Susan's marriage and extended family relationships is obedience to God's Word. They refused to see that their marriage needed Holy Scripture, which is "profitable for teaching, for reproof, for correction, for training in righteousness" (2 Timothy 3:16) to be faithfully applied to their emotions, wills, and temperaments.

It's apparent that neither of them were "doers of the word"; they were "merely hearers" (James 1:22).

Both Joseph and Susan failed to apply the teachings of Scripture to their personal lives, including their marital roles and extended family relationships. Their sinful behaviors and expressions of negative emotions within their marriage and with others contradict their claimed commitment to Christ and His Word. Their behavior showed that they were deceiving themselves, something James 1:22 warns us against.

If they were truly committed to Scripture and its application in their lives, how could Susan justify her shameful attitudes and outbursts of anger? How could she rationalize her treatment of others? How could Joseph defend his lack of spiritual leadership? What would Joseph and Susan's home be like if the biblical teachings on anger, love, humility, pride, patience, kindness, leadership, submission, the tongue, and selflessness were applied to their daily lives? I guarantee their marriage and relationships with Joseph's parents would look totally different.

> **In what area(s) of your life do you struggle most**
> **to apply biblical teaching?**

When I'm faced with counseling difficult sons- or daughters-in-law, without fail, they aren't applying God's Word to their everyday lives. They're living in a self-oriented world controlled by how they feel. Their self-centered justification, self-defensiveness, self-pity, self-righteousness, and self-worship control them and leave no room for any concern for others. That's what makes the relationship hell for their spouses and in-laws in particular.

Parents faced with such a son- or daughter-in-law need a lot of Holy Spirit enablement in order to tolerate such hypocritical behavior. If you respond to your son- or daughter-in-law using non-Christian tactics, he or she will feel justified in his or her mind for treating you poorly. On the other hand, a Christlike response will allow the Holy Spirit to work in your toxic son- or daughter-in-law's heart. That's the point of turning the other cheek when you are wronged—so the person who wronged you will take notice, that "they may see your good works, and glorify your Father who is in heaven" (Matthew 5:16). You may never be able to affect a toxic son- or daughter-in-law directly, but you can live a God-glorifying lifestyle and be an example of a loving Christ follower.

Below are a few passages that, when applied to marriage or any extended family relationship, will disarm disaster and make radical changes in relational outcomes. These passages contain Scripture principles that are relevant to everyone involved.

- **Attributes of Love:** "Love is patient, love is kind and is not jealous; love does not brag and is not arrogant, does not act unbecomingly; it does not seek its own, is not provoked, does not take into account a wrong suffered, does not rejoice in unrighteousness, but rejoices with the truth; bears all things, believes all things, hopes all things, endures all things" (1 Corinthians 13:4–8). The apostle Paul didn't just write this to take up space but was showing the Corinthian Church the "more excellent way" (1 Corinthians 12:31) of love, which is far superior to giftedness alone without love (1 Corinthians 13:1–3). Just imagine the effect that kind of love would have on Joseph and Susan's marriage. How different would their family relationships be?

> **Pause for a minute and consider how essential each attribute of love is to managing your toxic son- or daughter-in-law.**

• **Fruit of the Spirit:** "The fruit of the Spirit is love, joy, peace, patience, kindness, goodness, faithfulness, gentleness, self-control" (Galatians 5:22–23). When a person is serious about their walk with Christ and strives to be more like Christ, this fruit becomes evident in their life. The same would be true in Joseph and Susan's marriage and extended family. The absence of this fruit says a great deal about the condition of a person's walk with the Lord. This teaching will affect every person in the family.

• **Putting Off the Old Self, Putting On the New:** "Put them all aside: anger, wrath, malice, slander, and abusive speech from your mouth … Do not lie to one another … [Instead] put on a heart of compassion, kindness, humility, gentleness and patience; bearing with one another, and forgiving each other … Beyond all these things put on love" (Colossians 3:8–9, 12–14). "Let all bitterness and wrath and anger and clamor and slander be put away from you, along with all malice. Be kind to one another, tender-hearted, forgiving each other, just as God in Christ also has forgiven you" (Ephesians 4:31–32). This exercise of putting off and putting on would have helped the health of this family. We are not only to put off the sins of commission but also to put off the sins of omission. It's not just what we do to one another that causes disaster, but also what we fail to do for one another. We can all benefit from the application of this principle.

• **Fighting Hypocrisy:** "The one who says, 'I have come to know Him,' and does not keep His commandments, is a liar, and the truth is not in him; but whoever keeps His word, in him the love of God has truly been perfected. By this we know that we are in Him: the one who says he abides in Him *ought himself to walk in the same manner as He walked*" (1 John 2:4–6; italics added). We are to walk as Christ walked. That puts the bar up pretty high!

I mention these very familiar Scripture references on purpose. Most people have these verses underlined in their Bibles, maybe even memorized. But when it comes down to applying the Scriptures to our personal lives, we find it very difficult and often fail.

Children and parents alike, we should all strive to be obedient like my faithful cow dog. She would get scratched, kicked, and mistreated by the cows, but her obedience was useful to me, her master. Your toxic child-in-law may mistreat you. But remember that your obedience and faithfulness matter to your heavenly Master, Jesus Christ. Don't forget that disaster is disarmed when biblical patterns are faithfully, strategically, and intentionally lived out. How your biblical understanding is applied really matters.

If you respond to your son- or daughter-in-law using non-Christian tactics, he or she will feel justified in his or her mind for treating you poorly.

CHAPTER THIRTEEN

Disaster Minimized

What was missing from Joseph and Susan's marriage and family relationships? Yes, it was obedience to God's commands. They definitely had work to do in that area of their lives. But what about Joseph's parents? They seem to have maintained their Christian testimony, they weren't pushy, and they lived sacrificially for Joseph and Susan. I'm sure they tried to be helpful but must have understood their limits. It seems like they focused on obeying God's Word and loving their son and difficult daughter in-law the best way they could. I think they knew that they were both Christ-followers first and parents-in-law second. But you can bet they were constantly asking the question, "How can we minimize this disaster?"

Disaster is minimized when we "put on" Christ-honoring behavior. When we take the "high road" of selfless love and kindness, we minimize the disastrous results of having a toxic son- or daughter-in-law in our family relationships.

In Titus 2:6—8, Paul exhorts Titus, his son in the faith, to teach others to "be sensible; in all things show yourself to be an example of good deeds, with purity in doctrine, dignified, sound in speech which is beyond reproach, so that the opponent will be put to shame, having nothing bad to say about us." While this was instruction specifically to young men, it's also an exhortation to all of us, including fathers- and mothers-in-law.

In 1 John, the apostle makes the love of others a priority for a Christian:

- "Love one another" (3:11)

- "Love the brethren" (3:14)

- "We know love by this, that He laid down His life for us; and we ought to lay down our lives for the brethren" (3:16)

- "Everyone who loves is born of God and knows God" (4:7)

- "If God so loved us, we also ought to love one another" (4:11)

- "The one who abides in love abides in God" (4:16)

- "The one who loves God should love his brother also" (4:21)

As we have experienced the love of God, the natural result is for us to love others. However, we are often selective about who we love and who we don't. Our in-laws are often in the "don't love" category. This is very sad and unbiblical.

The apostle John reprimands those who don't live in love. In fact, it frightens me when I read John's descriptions of those who don't abide in a perpetual state of love. First John says a person "who does not love abides in death" (3:14), "does not know God" (4:8), "is a liar" and "cannot love God" (4:20).

I know what you're thinking. Some people are very difficult to be around, converse with, or have over for dinner. To sacrificially love those people is downright hard and can seem to be out of the question. But the fact that someone is difficult or annoying doesn't change the fact that we are to love them anyway. There are those, especially a toxic son- or daughter-in-law, who treat you poorly, criticize, judge, persecute, and even hate you, but the Bible is clear: we are to love our enemies and pray for those who persecute us (Matthew 5:44).

So you find it hard to love your son- or daughter-in-law. This may sound harsh, but so what? Does difficulty excuse you from reaching out to them through loving acts of kindness? Does their poor behavior give you an excuse not to be patient and understanding? Remember it's your God-given responsibility to love them.

Ask God to strengthen you to love the unlovely. The Bible gives many examples of those who loved the unlovely. Most importantly, Jesus loved us and "while we were yet sinners, Christ died for us" (Romans 5:8). Other examples include David's love for his wicked son Absalom, Joseph's love for his renegade brothers, the father's love for the prodigal son, the Good Samaritan's love for the injured Jewish man, as well as the Jewish and Gentile believers in the early church who loved each other.

I understand biblical love to be a matter of the will, not a response of the emotions. Furthermore, it's certainly not a biblical suggestion. It's a discipline, a volitional and intentional act. If we wait to love until we feel like it, we will never love. Unconditional love is not contingent on the other person's treatment of us. If this were the case, Jesus would never have died on the cross for us. Unconditional, Christlike love means turning the other cheek, forgiving, taking the blame, apologizing, or remaining silent—all done in love.

It's easy for us to react negatively to Susan. You might conclude it would be best for everyone if she was locked out of the house for a good period of time. But Joseph's entire family must remember to not fight, but instead be gentle, teachable, and tolerant to everyone (2 Timothy 2:25) including their toxic daughter-in-law.

In Titus, Paul instructs older men (fathers-in-law) to be "temperate, dignified, sensible, sound in faith, in love, in perseverance" and older women (mothers-in-law) to be "reverent ... not malicious gossips ... teaching what is good, so that they may encourage the young women to love their husbands, to love their children, to be sensible, pure, workers at home, kind, being subject to their own

husbands, so that the word of God will not be dishonored*
(Titus 2:2—5). I can assure you that "putting on" this kind
of behavior will minimize the disaster caused by a difficult
son- or daughter-in-law.

CHAPTER FOURTEEN

Disaster Contained

If it isn't the mice eating the chicken's food in the hen house, it's a dangerous mountain lion prowling around the ranch trying to eat my hens. The only way to avoid a shrinking number of hens is to lock them up in the hen house and not allow them to be loose in the barnyard. If my little hens run around outside of the hen house, they are in great danger of encountering the naughty lion who's looking for a warm meal. I like having my hens outside the hen house eating grass and feeding on bugs; it's good for them. Risky but good! If the lion got into the hen house, you can imagine the outcome—dead chickens and fewer eggs. So, a good rancher provides a pen where the chickens can be outside but protected by a nice wire enclosure.

One day, I looked out our kitchen window and saw a frustrated mountain lion peering through the wire enclosure at my hens. The hens were walking right along the wire fence tempting the mountain lion, knowing they were perfectly safe. In fact, you could see them stop and cluck-cluck at the lion as if to say, "Sorry, no lunch today!"

Many parents feel like a lion entered the family "hen house" when their son or daughter got married to a very difficult spouse. It wasn't Mom or Dad's choice, but it happened anyway. The dangerous lion came into the family and proceeded to make life disastrous for everyone with his or her nasty disposition. It's easy for us to talk of love, but when it comes right down to it, living a life of love can be very difficult—especially when the mountain lion is in the neighborhood and there are no wire enclosures. This might be why 1 John 3:18 gives an admonition we all need: "Let us not love with word or with tongue, but in deed and truth." Here are some questions to consider:

- What happens to your pursuit of godliness when a "lion" like Susan marries your son?

- How do you love "in deed and truth" when very difficult, stressful, and hurtful things happen?

- How can you "not be overcome by evil, but overcome evil with good" (Romans 12:21)?

- How might setting some boundaries be helpful?

Let's look at Joseph's parents again. I'm sure they tried to be helpful, but they also must have understood there must be some kind of limits, boundaries, or fences. They knew that attempting to correct Susan's behavior was a bad idea. In fact, it really wasn't their place to do so (Joseph was the one who should tackle that assignment, but by his own admission he had failed tragically). Great care must be given by the parents to not cause even more issues with Susan by confronting her behavior or setting an agenda for getting her help. That would be like me trying to talk the mountain lion out of eating my chickens—pretty silly and dangerous to say the least.

Many parents are pushy and feel it's their right and duty to deal with their adult child and difficult son- or daughter-in-law's marital or emotional issues. I just don't agree. Having a confrontational conversation with your adult child and your toxic in-law can have serious implications.

Instead, think boundaries and fences. There are many other people who can and will be more effective counseling your adult children and your toxic son- or daughter-in-law. Maybe a family friend could help, or another couple, a pastor, or family counselor. They're just "safer" and it keeps the lion (the toxic in-law and resulting problems) out of the original family unit or "hen house." Using outside help is a healthy boundary or fence for protection. It helps the parents avoid hurtful or threatening conversations with a difficult son- or daughter-in-law.

Furthermore, the mere fact that Dad and Mom are aware of Joseph's situation with Susan can start a dangerous chain of events. Being concerned parents is one thing, but taking charge of the healing process is quite another. It's nearly impossible for parents to remain neutral, impartial, and objective. They will naturally side with their son or daughter. Bottom line, great care should be given by everyone involved to avoid this dangerous terrain. Think boundary or fence. Rest assured, what a parent says about their child-in-law will get back to them, one way or another. So my advice is to tread lightly and be careful what you say!

I know what I'm suggesting is difficult. It goes against our instincts as parents. We want to protect our child from the mountain lion. But that's why we trust God who leads us by the Holy Spirit, enables us, and empowers us to do the difficult things. It's the Spirit who will empower you to keep your mouth shut instead of criticizing or trying to intervene in your child's marital problems. Our job as parents is to focus on living obediently to God's Word and learning the value of fences or boundaries for our protection.

The fence I put up around my chicken pen not only protected my chickens, it also kept in check the lion's nasty attitude and the damage he could do. Containment fences or boundaries work two ways. They protect us and also limit the hurt that can be inflicted upon us by others. Disaster in our families can be contained by implementing helpful boundaries for the benefit of all involved. I'll leave you with just a few boundaries for consideration.

1. **Don't allow yourself to think it's your responsibility to discipline or correct the toxic attitudes of your son- or daughter-in-law.** Your Christian attitude and sacrificial love are more apt to be "caught than taught." Stay out of difficult discussions where an insecure or defensive son- or daughter-in-law might become threatened, angry, or overreact. Remember Proverbs 15:1—"A gentle answer turns away wrath."

2. **Refuse to talk directly or counsel with your adult child and spouse about their marriage or extended family problems.** Generally, it's wise to refer them to someone else, since you're probably going to be somewhat partial and defensive. Strive to stay out of the counseling role with your adult child's marital problems. Use other resources.

3. **Try to understand the misdirected intentions of your toxic child-in-law.** As parents, we must understand our role and the unspoken intentions of the "lion" who seeks to bring disaster into our lives. This can include isolating your adult child from family and friends, or trying to control everything about your adult child, including their relationship with you, the parents. It can mean manipulating everyone and every situation.

In all of this, you must remain very flexible and cooperative. The son- or daughter-in-law that now is a part of your family has a lot of growing-up to do. It will take time, so be patient and, by God's grace, "wise as serpents and innocent as doves."

Part Four

It's About "Time"

CHAPTER FIFTEEN

While Time Marches On

At this point in the book, I know you're probably wanting to point out to me that many fathers- or mothers-in-law are pretty hard to get along with, that it isn't just the son- or daughter-in-law. And sometimes that's true. Believe me, I've counseled a whole bunch of them! However, the reason I'm writing this book and telling these stories is because there are some fathers- and mothers-in-law who are different. I've carefully selected the stories of those who aren't overbearing, bossy, pushy, or overly outspoken. Rather, I'm focusing on devoted, Christ-honoring parents who are simply caught in a horrible situation and looking for some practical guidance.

The next story will affirm what I'm saying. As you read on, notice how the parents, Tom and Kary, are interested in serving (as they do in every other area of their Christian journey). However, their toxic daughter-in-law (who professes to be a Christian) rejects, verbally abuses, dishonors, and disgraces them. For these parents, while time marches on, there seems to be no end in sight to this problem.

Thanks for the opportunity to tell our story regarding our daughter-in-law, Angie. We're not tattling, just trying to help other families experiencing a similar crisis. I hope our story will be helpful.

The first day I met Angie, I knew something was not right. She came over to our house with our son Blake but never once offered to help either in dinner preparation or clean-up. I guessed she was hesitant or reluctant and didn't know quite how to fit in—I'll grant her that. But when she didn't even say "thanks" for the dinner or offer a single positive comment about our home or hospitality, I began to sense something wasn't right. Most of the time, she sat alone thumbing through a pile of magazines, ignoring everyone including my son, her date. It seemed so strange.

Should Tom and Kary share specifics of their concerns with Blake?

As we spent more time with Angie, we found she was unkind, bossy, and cold. We also learned along the way that Angie came from a broken home. Her parents divorced when she was 6. She allegedly suffered some physical abuse from her father and brother while growing up. Her teen years were marked by anger, lies, and self-destructive behaviors. It was a heartbreaking story.

It's wonderful how God reaches out to hurting people like Angie. Her very first roommate at college was a Christian gal from California, who had a real influence on Angie. Praise God, Angie became a Christian and joined a campus ministry. (That's where she met Blake.)

> **What kinds of repercussions could her parents' divorce and abuse have had on Angie? Did these early traumas in her life bring about her need for control and self-protection?**

But as we spent more time with Angie, our anxiety over her relationship with Blake grew. We were genuinely concerned. We cautiously tried to slow things down. We thought Blake needed to observe Angie's behavior, notice her emotional struggles, and get some outside advice. But Blake and Angie made every excuse for not getting outside counseling. Both of them were too busy with school work and their social lives, they said. They were fast approaching the marriage altar, and we couldn't do a thing about it.

The wedding was a huge disappointment. We saw a side of Angie that had previously gone undetected. Angie exploded at people in fits of rage again and again during the wedding events. She was rude to both of us and didn't want our participation in any of the activities. It was just horrible. We paid for their honeymoon to Europe, but no sooner had they returned when Blake informed us there was a problem. The honeymoon had been a disaster due to Angie's out-of-control rage. It was then that Blake confessed this was a problem even while they were dating, but he'd thought she would get over it after the wedding. Of course, he was hoping she would mature in this area. But that wasn't happening.

How should Blake respond when Angie blows up? Do you think he noticed how Angie mistreated his parents?

Not long after they were married, things escalated even more. Angie started hitting, kicking, and biting Blake. At one point, it got so bad that he called the police. We were horrified to learn she had actually threatened to kill him. After that, they separated for several months and sought outside help. I'm ashamed to confess, I wished they would get divorced. I was so terrified that Angie would do something terrible to my son!

What contact would you recommend between Blake and Angie during the separation?

However, Blake and Angie eventually got back together, had another child, and for work reasons moved out of town. We now see them occasionally but not near as often as earlier in their marriage. The distance now makes visiting difficult, but we stay in touch as much as possible. In fact, we were hopeful that our relationship with Angie was gradually improving.

> Could stricter boundaries on Kary's end help the situation? Would it be a viable option for Kary to stay in a motel when visiting instead of being under Angie's feet 24/7?

Well, recent events showed that was wishful thinking! Shortly after their second baby was born, I went to assist Angie with the new baby (just a couple of weeks old) and her older brother (4 years old). The plan was for me to stay a couple of nights with Angie while Blake was out of town on a work assignment. It turned out to be a disaster. I really tried to be helpful . . . providing transportation, cooking, cleaning, and grocery shopping. I just wanted to help Angie and care for our grandson while she adjusted to the new baby. I had no hidden agenda. But Angie was never thankful for my help, and frequently exploded in anger.

It all came to a head a few days in. The baby was having some digestive issues and was fussy. My grandson and I returned from running errands and found Angie beside herself and extremely stressed over the screaming, sick baby. She said to me that she couldn't deal with it anymore. After her frequent physical abuse of my son, I was concerned about Angie's emotional state and the safety of the baby. So I chose my words carefully and said, "Angie, do you think we should take her to the hospital?" She exploded immediately, yelling, "How dare you! Get out!"

Why doesn't it help the situation if Blake says nothing when Angie attacks his parents? Why is Blake afraid to take the leadership in his marriage?

I started packing up my belongings, all the while being criticized and verbally abused. (I wouldn't speak to my dog the way she yelled at me.) I was almost out the door when my grandson grabbed my leg and begged to go with me. The situation was so volatile I decided to stay for my grandson's sake and kept my mouth shut. When Blake returned home, Angie told him I was no longer welcome at their home because I had undermined her parenting. I'm not justifying anything I did or didn't do but nothing deserved her hateful and self-centered response.

There's an element of truth in the old adage "no good deed goes unpunished" because Angie punishes me for most things I do for her. This trip was no exception; rather, it is just one of many illustrations of our relationship with Angie for the last 10 years.

We've always had a very good and special relationship with Blake and we want to keep it that way, but Angie makes it very difficult. We call him on his cell phone so we can talk to him alone. Otherwise Angie demands our calls must be on the speaker phone. Let me tell you something, she is a master manipulator and control freak! She controls every aspect of our relationship with the grandchildren. We long for a close and loving relationship with them, but we can't have one because Angie sees it as a threat and lashes out. She maintains an insanely strict schedule for the children. Boy, do we get in trouble if we don't adhere precisely to the schedule as she orders! Blake is caught in the middle, but in order to stay out of trouble, he gives in to Angie's demands. Frankly, I think he's enabling her bad, controlling disposition. At the very least, he's stuck with two children he loves and a very difficult wife. I often reflect on how they met and regret Blake's lack of discernment in marrying her. I guess it's often true that "love is blind."

> **How could Blake reconcile the fact that Angie claimed to be a Christian and yet acted in such hateful ways to other people?**

There is such sadness in all of this. We grieve for the grandchildren. Presently, there are no signs of physical abuse of them, but plenty of signs of verbal abuse. Our grandson is frightened by his mom's screaming fits and obeys out of total fear. It troubles me that Blake will never know selfless, sacrificial love from this difficult woman. I fear for my grandchildren and their emotional well-being.

I work hard to not be angry, to accept this whole situation as from the Lord, and to trust that time heals. But, it is so hard to see my son and grandchildren suffer under Angie's constant emotional struggles. — Kary

---

Well, there you have it—another story of a self-centered, self-justifying, self-willed daughter-in-law and a husband who's apparently unable or too fearful to challenge her sinful behavior, leaving his parents in a very uncomfortable situation. In Psalm 31:15, David says, "My times are in Your hand; deliver me from the hand of my enemies and from those who persecute me." He took comfort knowing that God was in total control of his life, even in difficult times. Tom and Kary take comfort in the same promise. Though they continue to experience uncertain times with an enemy right in their family, they are trusting God as time marches on.

CHAPTER SIXTEEN

A Time For Prayer

I know most of my readers have never considered what it's like to break a young horse to ride. A few may have tried and been successful, but most of us who have tried struggled to succeed and sometimes in the process ended up in a heap, needing medical care. Breaking a horse is not an easy assignment but one that's necessary, especially on a ranch. I'll give you an example of how I go about it.

Breaking in a horse to ride starts when the horse is really young. The first step is putting a halter on his little head along with a 6- to 8-foot lead rope. He must learn to follow. The young critter doesn't like this very much, but over several days, after some bucking, pulling, and jerking he eventually learns to follow the old cowboy on the other end of the rope. Let me emphasize—it doesn't happen overnight. All of this takes lots of time and effort.

After a couple of years, the little colt has turned into a pretty sizable horse called a gelding (castrated horse).

It's now time to introduce the gelding to a bridle and saddle. All of this equipment is new, invasive, and constrictive for the horse so I carefully slip the bit into his mouth while lifting the bridle over his ears, and then cinch down the saddle around his belly. It doesn't matter what kinds of gimmicks are used; it takes a lot of patience and a lot of time before the ornery gelding accepts his new equipment.

After he's accustomed to the bridle and saddle, this old cowboy puts his boot in the stirrup, swings his leg over the saddle and holds on for dear life. As soon as my rear end lands in the saddle the gelding goes nuts, bucking, jumping, twisting, and turning, I generally go flying through the air trying to locate my hat. After picking myself up off the ground and out of the cow pies, there's a renewed resolve that the gelding isn't going to win this contest. The horse also has his own, very different resolve, so when this old cowboy gets on again he's in for another bumpy ride. The goal is to keep my feet in the stirrups, my rear in the saddle and my teeth in my mouth; then chances are I can outlast the bucking, twisting, and snorting that will take place. If I can successfully stick to my resolve, the young gelding will eventually adjust and allow me to just sit in the saddle and relax.

Through my experiences breaking young horses, I've learned that patience and treating the horse with respect are essential to developing a good saddle animal. If you use anger, sticks, or whips, your difficulties will increase proportionately. If you scream or yell, it will only make things worse. A cowboy is much better off if he uses his brain to outsmart the feisty gelding.

It's the same with sons- and daughters-in-law. You must move patiently, slowly, and respectfully, or the job will be increasingly more difficult. And you must use your brain when dealing with them. Acting in ignorance, on impulse, or out of anger will lead to a very bumpy relationship, and you might end upside down in the kitchen.

With that story in mind, let's consider some of the options available to Tom and Kary in dealing with their daughter-in-law. I'm sure there are many times when Tom would like to give Angie a stern "talking-to" or take her out back of the barn (like an old cowboy might consider doing to a headstrong gelding). But neither of those would work. You see, Tom and Kary are in a very difficult and delicate position. If they put their foot down and refuse to tolerate Angie's frustrating attitude, they run the risk of losing their son and grandchildren permanently. This would make Angie very happy because she wouldn't need to share Blake and the children with them any longer.

Should Tom do something to protect his wife from Angie's combative personality? Is there ever a time when Tom should step in to defend his son, grandchildren, or Kary from abusive Angie?

So instead of lashing out or trying to control Angie's disposition, Tom and Kary have chosen to set aside their hurt and sadness, accept the situation, smile, keep their mouths shut and pray. They hold on to the hope that things can change and that their relationships will improve. They continue to be kind to Angie and treat her respectfully. They make sure they always show love to their son and keep an open door for him to call or reach out to them if he needs their help. They can only do this because they are constantly leaning on the Lord in faith and in prayer.

Angie's anger and unhappiness have driven them both to a deeper prayer life—especially Kary, who has borne the brunt of Angie's abuse. They've made a habit of praying faithfully about the situation remembering that prayer should be a priority in times like these. Let's consider some special prayer needs that might be helpful to Tom and Kary in their struggle with Blake and Angie's situation.

1. **Pray for a Christlike response to your feelings and emotions.**
   It's natural to feel sadness, disappointment, hurt, and frustration in these kinds of situations. Clearly Tom and Kary are being treated wrongly! And it's easy to let those feelings turn into anger or other sinful attitudes toward the toxic son- or daughter-in-law. It's also extremely tempting to give vent to your feelings to others in your family or to friends. Kary has told me she makes every effort to take her sadness and frustration to the Lord through prayer, not

to Blake. We must actively give our pain and fear over to the Lord and trust Him to take care of the situation. Pray about your emotions and how you respond in the situation. Remember, "The Lord is near to the brokenhearted and saves those who are crushed in spirit" (Psalm 34:18).

2. **Pray for a positive attitude.** It's so easy to slip into negativity. Be careful about speaking negatively in front of your grandchildren or other family members and friends. This is one of the most difficult things to practice. A positive attitude is so important. It communicates a trust in God, that He can bring about the desired changes. I'm reminded of Proverbs 15:13, 15: "A joyful heart makes a cheerful face, but when the heart is sad, the spirit is broken…A cheerful heart has a continual feast." A spirit of hopefulness and trust in God are essential to quiet negative dispositions. We need to focus on the good areas of life and the little blessings God gives each day.

3. **Pray for patience.** Patience is the great need in these trying situations. We want quick and permanent change, but that seldom happens. We need patience to endure. Psalm 37:7 says, "Rest in the Lord and wait patiently for Him; do not fret because of him who prospers in his way, because of the man [or woman] who carries out wicked schemes." So, ask God to give you patience while you wait.

4. **Pray for protection.** When people get angry, that's when emotional, spiritual, and physical abuse can occur, especially in already dysfunctional relationships. Children and other family members need protection from the hurtful attitudes and actions of a toxic son- or daughter-in-law. Parents should also be careful to not be hurtful in any attitude or action. So pray for protection for everyone involved. Psalm 56:3–4 says, "When I am afraid, I will put my trust in You. In God, whose word I praise, in God I have put my trust; I shall not be afraid. What can mere man do to me?"

5. **Pray for heart change.** Don't just pray for the situation to change; pray for God to help everyone mature and to change the hearts of everyone involved (including ourselves). As the Bible says, it is "out of the abundance of the heart the mouth speaks. A good man out of the good treasure of his heart brings forth good things, and an evil man out of the evil treasure brings forth evil things" (Matthew 12:34–35 NKJV). Therefore, we must mature and guard our hearts. So pray for genuine heart change, and then pray that the situation would change as a result.

6. **Pray for strength to trust God.** Leaving our burden with the Lord is a volitional action we all must take. And we can pray for strength to keep doing that every day. Here are some verses to keep in the forefront of our minds:

Trust in the Lord and do good ... Delight yourself in the Lord; and He will give you the desires of your heart. Commit your way to the Lord, trust also in Him, and He will do it. He will bring forth your righteousness as the light. (Psalm 37:3–6)

Do not let your heart be troubled; believe in God, believe also in Me. (John 14:1)

Thus says the Lord, "Let not a wise man boast of his wisdom, and let not the mighty man boast of his might, let not a rich man boast of his riches; but let him who boasts boast of this, that he understands and knows Me, that I am the Lord who exercises lovingkindness, justice and righteousness on earth, for I delight in these things," declares the Lord. (Jeremiah 9:23–24)

I've been involved with Tom and Kary and their situation for many years. I've tried to give you a glimpse into their hearts to see their faith in action. I hope you can appreciate their love expressed in self-control and not seeking their own way (1 Corinthians 13:5). Furthermore, I hope you grasp their commitment to prayer and the strength they draw from a merciful God. Unlike so many parents, this couple's God is very big and capable of making changes to their relationship with Blake and Angie. However, the process is very, very slow as God works His will into the lives of His beloved children. In the meantime, Tom and Kary make time for prayer, extending love to Angie and Blake, smiling a lot, staying positive, and being very, very patient just like the old cowboy does when breaking a young horse.

CHAPTER SEVENTEEN

It All Takes Time

As a rancher, I've trained all kinds of critters to be nice to me—dogs, cats, parakeets, horses, cows, a couple of deer, a raccoon, and a fox. My favorite, however, was a wild dog. When I first met "Black Dog," I was down at the barn and he was in the lower pasture by the creek. For several mornings I saw him down by the creek, but he wouldn't come anywhere near the barn. After milking the cows, I always had some milk left. One morning, I started taking some milk down to the creek and leaving it for Black Dog. He would hide until I walked back to the barn, then he would come out and drink the milk.

I kept this up, and gradually started moving the bucket closer and closer to the barn. Black Dog continued to come for the milk. Our relationship was improving! But I wanted to make sure I didn't scare off Black Dog. I pretended to ignore him and never made eye contact, so he would feel safe.

Eventually, the day came when the bucket was just inside the barn, right next to my milking stool. With great hesitation, Black Dog came closer to have a drink and then jumped back out of the barn. He continued this back-and-forth motion for a while. I continued to avoid eye contact, but I started talking to him as he jumped back and forth. Eventually he settled down and got his milk. But we never had any physical contact and I still had all ten fingers. Life was good!

A while after that, we progressed to the point where I could squirt some warm milk right from the cow on his nose. Boy, did he like that! He'd open his mouth, wanting a bigger squirt. Soon, I started squirting some milk onto my boot for him to lick. After that, I squirted some onto my hand, hoping he'd give me a lick and smell my hand.

Well, it was smooth sailing after that. Once he smelled my hand, Black Dog realized I wasn't his old abusive owner but a safe rancher who needed a friend. He trounced all around the ranch with me for several years, until his injuries from a bad accident forced me to put him down. That was a very sad day; Black Dog was a great friend and companion.

As with Black Dog, winning the heart of a difficult son- or daughter-in-law takes time, maybe even a lifetime. Occasionally, these difficult folks come from very complicated backgrounds. Like Black Dog, they're afraid, insecure, and angry, and they are tired of getting kicked around. But deep down inside, they still want to be loved, understood, and treated with compassion and respect.

For wise fathers- and mothers-in-law, the process is long and arduous. Don't expect your son- or daughter-in-law to instantly feel safe with your family. You must reach out to them in gentleness with a little milk. Whatever you do, don't be aggressive. Remember Black Dog. Over time they'll come a little closer, providing you don't scare them away with your words or actions. Your efforts to love them and make them feel comfortable are never wasted. Those self sacrificing efforts will pay dividends but maybe not as rapidly as you would like, so be patient. Remember, time is on your side, so don't rush it.

But, "What if Black Dog had bitten you on the hand? you might ask. If that happened, I would say I must have moved too quickly, and Black Dog wasn't ready for that level of intimacy. I might have to go back to the bucket for a while. The same is true in human relationships. Sometimes our expectations for our son- or daughter-in-law are too much for them. Sometimes we can get pushy when we need to take our time and relax.

Let's get some biblical perspective. When you have a son or daughter-in-law acting like Black Dog, some biblical perspective is always helpful. The apostle Paul writes about the marks of a Christian in Romans 12:9–21, reminding us of some very important principles for managing and untangling difficult relationships that have soured, become strained, or reached a stalemate. Take a look at what Paul says and how they apply to family relationships:

1. "Let love be without hypocrisy" — Don't try to fake it. Your in-law will see through it if you do!

2. "Be devoted to one another in brotherly [family] love" — Even if they are really tough to love.

3. "Give preference to one another in honor" — Show respect and look for the good in people.

4. "Not lagging behind in diligence, [but] fervent in spirit" — This process takes strategy, creativity, commitment, and perseverance.

5. "Rejoicing in hope, persevering in tribulation" — Family life is tough stuff. But don't give up hope. Remember it is God you are trusting in.

6. "Devoted to prayer" — It's important to understand God's role in the healing process.

7. "Practicing hospitality" — Continue to reach out and find ways to show love, even when it's difficult or frightening.

8. "Bless those who persecute you" — This includes difficult sons- or daughters-in-law.

9. "Rejoice with those who rejoice, and weep with those who weep" — Don't let a vengeful attitude steal your empathy.

10. "Be of the same mind toward one another" — Even with those who aren't the most harmonious.

11. "Do not be haughty ... Do not be wise in your own estimation" — Pride always comes before a fall, and no one likes being around a proud person. Besides, you have nothing to boast about.

12. "Never pay back evil for evil to anyone" — Don't be reactive.

13. "If possible, so far as it depends on you, be at peace with all men" — You can be at peace even when others aren't. Peace is first a heart issue.

14. "Do not be overcome by evil, but overcome evil with good" — Jesus said being kind to your enemy is like heaping coals of fire on their head. Don't forget that it's by good works that God is glorified (Matthew 5:16).

Here's a very significant principle to keep in mind if, as a parent, you respond to your son- or daughter-in-law in a negative and unchristian manner, your son- or daughter-in-law will easily justify his or her sinful behavior toward you as a result. Let the Holy Spirit work on your son- or daughter in-law, and focus on not getting in the Spirit's way by your unkind behavior. All of this takes a lot of time.

For wise fathers- and mothers-in-law, the process is long and arduous. Don't expect your son- or daughter-in-law to instantly feel safe with your family.

CHAPTER EIGHTEEN

Using Time Wisely

Time is a crazy commodity and is measured in seconds, minutes, hours, days, weeks, months, years, and a lifetime. People run out of time and question "where did the time go?" Sometimes we say, "time goes so slowly," and other times, we "don't have enough time." We're all taught not to "waste our time." With such varying thoughts and reactions to time, how can we really understand the value of this thing called "time"?

I've always told my children that time is on our side. In other words, be patient, don't rush it, make the most of it. Generally speaking, there's always more time, another time, or a better time—not for procrastinating but for productivity. There'll be time for rest, time for study, time for prayer, friends, and family, but there's "no time like the present." Charles Buxton says it this way: "You'll never find time for anything. If you want time, you must make it."

Then there is what I call the more seasonal use of the word "time." The wise Solomon says there is a time "for every event under heaven" — "time to plant," "time to weep," "time to embrace," "time to love," etc.—throughout the book of Ecclesiastes. It's not measured in minutes or days, but in seasons or events.

Tom and Kary are experiencing a time in their lives they didn't plan on, hoped would never happen, and pray will end soon. As you recall their story, you probably realize the end was not even in sight for them. Their daughter-in-law is a long-term headache they have to deal with. Plowing through the daily nightmare that had become their family relationships was so disruptive and frustrating to everyone. What was once a family with great fellowship became a family fractured, broken, and in need of relief.

During our lives, there are times when we experience trials and suffering, sickness, discouragement, depression, and failure. I'm counseling with families that are in the grip of a terminal cancer diagnosis, parents with a disabled child, families hurting from an accidental death of a loved one, and others clinging to a broken marriage. These are all painful times or seasons of life.

When we find ourselves in times like these, how do we maintain our Christlike testimony? How do we get through the next month, year, or decade while the difficult situation continues?

In Ephesians 5:15–16, Paul the great apostle instructs Christians this way: "Therefore be careful how you walk, not as unwise men but as wise, making the most of your time, because the days are evil." In Colossians 4:5, we are told, "Conduct yourselves with wisdom toward outsiders, making the most of the opportunity." In other words, we are to make the most of the time allowed us by fulfilling God's purposes and using every opportunity, even if these are challenging and hurtful, for His glory and the spread of His gospel.

There are times in our lives when things just don't make sense, or they don't seem to fit with other times in our lives. But as Christians, we've seen enough of God's power, wisdom, and love to believe with good reason that, in the end, the pieces of our lives do actually fit together even if, in the moment, we have our doubts. Just review the life of Joseph found in Genesis 37–42. His circumstances weren't on his wish list either. He was put in a pit, sold as a slave by his brothers, falsely accused by a married woman, put in prison, and forgotten by a couple of cell mates. Eventually, though, all the pieces came together just as God planned.

So be encouraged by Romans 8:28, "We know that God causes all things to work together for good to those who love God, to those who are called according to His purpose." When the details in your life don't seem to fit together, and relationships don't pan out as you'd hoped, just remember that God is working in the details to accomplish His great purpose in your life and family.

Our passage in Ephesians tells us to watch carefully how we live, be alert, be vigilant. Apply wisdom to make the most of your time because the "days are evil," the opposition is great. In other words, watch your steps, be smart, and don't miss the opportunity to live for Christ. In order to make the most of your time and not miss an opportunity, here are a couple of suggestions.

- **Understand your time is short.** Psalm 90:12 says, "Teach us to number our days." If we don't understand how short our time is, we won't make the most of it and opportunities for spiritual service will be missed. These opportunities include such things as cultivating relationships, serving in ministry, or growing our biblical understanding.

- **Plan your time strategically.** Proverbs 21:5 says, "The plans of the diligent lead surely to advantage, but everyone who is hasty comes surely to poverty." We must prayerfully and strategically set short-term and long-term goals in order to maximize opportunities that come our way. For example, Tom and Kary could plan outings around the interests of Angie and Blake. Or they could make it their goal not to call as often. A long-term goal might be to avoid counterproductive discussions and debates, and avoid giving unwanted parenting advice. A short-term goal might be as simple as attempting to have a warm and kind greeting when Blake and Angie arrive.

- **Make the best use of your time.** Making the most of our time can mean "redeeming" or "buying back" opportunities. In other words, it can mean giving up other things we could do, in order to maximize the best use of our time. In troublesome relationships, it's sometimes better to have something planned so you don't end up sitting around looking at each other. Play a game, enjoy an outside event, or engage in some form of recreation like fishing or knitting. Use your time to enrich your relationships. Don't just sit around and watch TV.

- **Protect your time by avoiding evil.** Sin is the biggest waste of time and effort. We live in a world filled with evil and the temptation to compromise spiritual values. It's always knocking on our door. Falling into sinful actions and attitudes within family conflicts results in harmful consequences and loss of valuable time.

Wise fathers- and mothers-in-law who make the most of their time are characterized by sacrificial living, pursuing Christlikeness, growing healthy relationships, and always learning, understanding, and doing God's will; whereas the fool wastes spiritual opportunities. We should take advantage of every opportunity to demonstrate Christ to our family by being an example in word and in deed. Your toxic son- or daughter-in-law should always be able to see in you sacrificial kindness, a willingness to help when asked, a compromising spirit, a balanced attitude even under stress, a trust in God, and a humble heart even when being mistreated. For those struggling in difficult times, let me comfort and encourage you with these lyrics from an old hymn:

> In times like these you need a Savior,
> In times like these you need an anchor;
> Be very sure, be very sure,
> Your anchor holds and grips the Solid Rock!
>
> In times like these you need the Bible,
> In times like these, O be not idle;
> Be very sure, be very sure,
> Your anchor holds and grips the Solid Rock!

("In Times Like These," music and lyrics by Ruth C. Jones)

In what ways could Tom and Kary waste valuable time and opportunities?

Part Five

It Makes Me So Angry!

CHAPTER
NINETEEN

A Family Affair

If you haven't noticed, most difficult sons- or daughters-in-law firmly believe they are never wrong, always think of themselves as the victim, and personalize every negative comment. I don't think there's a more frustrating situation for a parent or family member to be in. Remember, you didn't choose them, they chose your child to marry. As the saying goes, "You can choose your friends, but you can't choose your family." As you observe your son- or daughter-in-law's know-it-all attitude, angry outbursts, and critical treatment of your family members, you want to support, help, and, at times, defend your son or daughter against their toxic attack. But you find yourself in an enormous pickle.

If you say anything, you're accused of sticking your nose where it doesn't belong, or of taking sides with your son or daughter. But if you don't say anything, your toxic son- or daughter-in-law will be convinced you can't communicate, or that you don't care. What's interesting to me is that such accusations are laid at the feet of many fathers- or mothers-in-law who have very meaningful relationships with countless other people in their social circles and are very good communicators at church or work and with other family members. And they obviously care about the situation and their child and his or her spouse. The fact is, they don't dare communicate for fear of running into a human buzz saw—their son- or daughter-in-law who is actually the one incapable of carrying on normal, non-threatening relationships. The following reflection from Tony will help illustrate this point.

So far in this book, I've focused on how this affects the parents-in-law, but I should point out that a toxic son- or daughter-in-law will also affect the rest of the family, particularly other siblings. This dilemma—wanting to help, defend, or intervene in some way but knowing the additional problems that could cause—is not something just the parents face. It's faced by the siblings of the individual who's married to the toxic person. I've briefly mentioned siblings in some of the previous stories, but here's Tony's story from the perspective of a brother-in-law.

I am writing to you about my older brother Max and his wife Jessie. Let me start by saying my parents love each other and have always set a good example for us. I have five siblings, all of whom are married. Max is the oldest of my siblings. I thoroughly enjoy most of my brothers- and sisters-in-law.

They're all respectful of my parents and do a fine job raising their children. Then there's my brother Max and his crazy wife Jessie.

Before Max and Jessie married, I didn't really know her very well and didn't have an opinion about her, one way or the other. After their wedding, I found out that Jessie's parents had divorced when she was a teenager, and that she had struggled a lot with that, but it seemed to be an issue she'd dealt with. Things seemed fine. Jessie had joined our family, and it was no big deal.

During the first year of their marriage, Jessie was usually thankful and glad to be a part of our healthy family. But other times, she was downright resentful and jealous of our close family and defensive of her broken family. This tension seemed to increase, and after a while, Jessie began to distance herself from the rest of us. This hurt my parents a lot because they were very inviting and loving to Jessie and welcomed her with open arms. I think Jessie was angry because the love we expressed within our family was missing in her family of origin. I think she wanted that same kind of love from her own family, but wasn't receiving it. I think this depressed her and made her resentful toward us. That's just my opinion.

How do you react to Tony's comments about why Jessie was angry? Do you agree?

From the beginning, Jessie was a lot like me—a strong-headed, alpha-type personality. This personality trait began to cause problems in Max and Jessie's marriage. You couldn't help but witness the tension between them, and I often thanked God I wasn't married to Jessie. Problems between them escalated, and you could easily conclude Jessie was an extremely angry and difficult person. She had a very short temper and was generally rude. Poor Max! He'd make excuses to us for her behavior, saying she was tired or hungry. Max spent a lot of time dancing around her ups and downs.

Imagine our family gatherings: everyone walking around very gingerly, making small talk, and trying not to ruffle Jessie's feathers for fear she would get "ticked" and explode. Frankly, everyone was always tense and uncomfortable when she was around. She was so opinionated about everything, it became nauseating, and you didn't dare disagree. Her way was always the only way. Whenever Jessie felt she was mistreated by someone or didn't get what she deserved, she would rudely confront that person in public. I remember hearing about one especially embarrassing incident when all of the mothers (sisters and sisters-in-law) took their children (15 in total) to the mall to go shopping. Something about the price and the quality of service triggered Jessie to lose control and get angry at the store staff. Her sisters-in-law were all humiliated and upset by her horrible display of anger.

What would be a softer approach to a disagreement over poor service?

My own relationship with Jessie went downhill quickly when she left Max and sought legal separation. It wasn't until then that Max confided in me how Jessie really treated him. At one point, she had told Max that she hoped he would "die in a car accident. It would simplify their separation." When I heard this, I was so mad, I could no longer sit back and do nothing about Jessie's behavior. Her treatment of my brother was atrocious, and she needed to be confronted. Here's the problem. I had already been nursing a serious dislike of Jessie. I knew as a Christian it wasn't acceptable, but I'd had it up to my neck with her toxic personality.

My angry state didn't help our communication nor my email correspondence. Initially, I asked questions and tried to get Jessie's side of the story, but our communication quickly escalated into angry phone calls, unpleasant confrontations, and her predictable denial of any fault whatsoever. If I'd insinuate to Jessie that she played a role in their failed marriage, she would hang up the phone. Jessie's mother even came to her defense using "unchristian" voice mails with several one-syllable words.

If she were a true Christian, what role should Jessie's mother play in this situation?

Eventually I reached a point where I sincerely wanted the whole family to reconcile and was willing to do whatever was necessary to make it happen, including asking for forgiveness for my previous outbursts. I just wanted to help Jessie understand what her behavior was doing to her husband and children. In desperation, I contacted Jessie's mother and Jessie via email and tried to explain to them why I thought Jessie's actions were unacceptable and how I felt Jessie's family was enabling her bad behavior. As you can imagine, this email went over like a lead balloon and only served to further inflame the relationship between myself and Jessie. The tension got worse between Jessie's parents and our family.

Was Tony on the right path?
What would you do differently?

Here's the issue for my family. I'm the more confrontational brother and desire to press forward with reconciliation in hurting relationships. I try to be patient and gentle, but it doesn't always come across that way. This is my fault.

I've observed that my other brother and sisters have all dealt with Jessie in different ways. One has displayed much more compassion, some have withdrawn from the situation because of anger toward Jessie, another sibling has chosen to stay away from Jessie and focus all her attention on Max. All of my siblings have struggled to know where our place is in this conflict. Should we continue to confront Jessie, cut off contact, or continue to show her love and pursue a relationship? Although we all desire (to some extent) reconciliation for Max and Jessie's marriage, we're fearful the bridges have been burned between ourselves and Jessie. We don't know what our extended family relationships would look like if Jessie and Max were to reconcile. — Tony

**What should the siblings do if Jessie and Max
get back together?**

As I am finishing this book, a very public illustration of how families—especially siblings—are affected by the arrival of new in-laws has been in the media.

Reporting on Britain's royal family, a Fox News article from November 2019 stated that "Numerous sources have long insisted there were deep tensions between the brothers after [Britain's Prince] Harry revealed to his family he wanted to marry the former American actress [Meghan Markle] after less than a year of dating. When William cautioned Harry that the whirlwind romance was moving too quickly, Harry reportedly became angry and hurt."

The article also reported that "'eyes are open' about the emotional distress the pair is enduring, but the relationship between the couple and the rest of the royal family hasn't grown closer.... They don't speak, no one is checking in."

Maybe I should send Prince William a copy of this book and remind him that it's often better to smile a lot, keep your mouth shut and pray instead of passing out unwanted opinions. Regardless of family status, whether you're a "royal" or a "regular" family, adding a daughter-in-law or son-in-law into the mix can cause a ROYAL mess.

Stephanie Nolasco, 2019, "Meghan Markle, Prince Harry's relationship with the royals hasn't changed, pal claims: 'They don't speak,'" Fox News, November 20, 2019; accessed December 6, 2019 from https://www.foxnews.com/entertainment/meghan-markle-prince-harry-royals-dont-speak

CHAPTER TWENTY

Fuses, Circuit Breakers, and Anger

B efore we dive deeper into Tony's story, let me tell you one of my own. A few years ago, we had had a very busy spring season, so my wife Nancy and I decided to take a quiet break in the Colorado mountains for a few days. We spent our time fishing, swimming, hiking, and just plain goofing off. It was a great trip, and we returned to the ranch totally relaxed. That is, until we entered our house around 10:30 pm after a long drive.

The minute we stepped in the back door, I knew we had a problem. I tried to turn on the porch light, but it didn't work. Must be a bulb burned out, right? Next, we tried the entry room light and it didn't work. Stumbling down the hallway to the kitchen area, we tried the kitchen lights. None of them worked either. The house was blacker than the inside of a cow, so I reached for my trusty LED flashlight, which was right next to the kitchen in my desk drawer. I did a fast trip through the house and not a single light worked, not even the one in the refrigerator.

I'm not an electrician, but I guessed the main circuit breaker must have gone out. Flashlight in hand, I headed for the scary gray box in the garage. Flipping up the lid was very intimidating, with approximately 30 circuit breakers staring me in the face and one big one at the top which shut off all power to the house. Every one of the circuit breakers appeared okay, but I turned each one "off" then "on" to make sure and went back into the house. Still no lights. Something was really "fishy," because I noticed that the barnyard lights were working.

With only a candle Nancy had lit and my small flashlight to guide us, we were in a real quandary. We had no clue what was wrong until Nancy went into our guest bedroom to check the lights in there. On the nightstand, she noticed the clock radio was showing the time in bright green numbers. This was strange since the clock radio was getting power, but the lights weren't. She shined my flashlight on the electrical socket where both the clock radio and table lamp were plugged in. How could this be she wondered? "It must be the light bulb," she thought.

It was then that she noticed the light bulb was missing. Further inspection revealed that every light bulb in the entire house (including the one in the refrigerator) was missing! It wasn't an electrical problem like a bad fuse or blown circuit breaker after all. Someone had maliciously stolen every one of our light bulbs in the entire house!

We went to bed that night in pitch darkness. The next morning, I went down to the barn to collect eggs from our chickens. There, hiding in the straw, were a dozen eggs and over 80 light bulbs! Later on, we found out this whole thing was a trick played on us by four gremlin grandchildren, our rascal daughter, and my creative son-in-law. This was a pretty good trick, but time is on my side. The next time they go on vacation, I think I'll probably remove all the toilets in their house and hang them in a tree out in the backyard. Think revenge!

––––––––––––––––––––––

Unlike the trick played on us, a fried fuse or blown circuit breaker can wreak havoc on any electrical system. Whenever an electrical short or something else bad happens in an electrical circuit, the fuse or circuit breaker either blows up or burns up, leaving you in the dark, stranded, or unable to cook bacon on the electric stove.

So many people are like fuses or circuit breakers. When things don't go just right, they "blow up" or "burn up" with anger. When you put two sinners together in marriage, add children who are sinners to the mix, and then top it off with a problematic son- or daughter-in-law, you have a sure-fire recipe for "overloaded emotional circuits" and "blown fuses,' more commonly known as "angry outbursts."

Dads and moms who are dealing with a toxic son- or daughter-in-law are some of the most susceptible to "blowing a fuse." Nothing is more aggravating than being abused, falsely accused, ignored, or rejected by a toxic in-law who also mistreats your son or daughter in the process. Honestly, it can be very infuriating, and it's very easy for a parent to eventually "blow their fuse."

I'll use another family squabble to illustrate and underscore what not to do in such a situation. Remember, there's a lot at stake if you mishandle either your emotions or your toxic son- or daughter-in-law.

Jerry and Ruth had a very difficult time with their daughter-in-law. She was self-focused, stubborn, and didn't fit very comfortably into the family. Jerry was a perfect example of how not to behave when your child marries a toxic daughter-in-law. I counseled with Jerry on and off for many years about his anger toward his son's wife, with little success. No question about it, Jerry's daughter-in-law was a very toxic personality and she said many hurtful things about Jerry. One day, his fuses blew, emotional circuits burned, and the relationship lights went dark. Jerry foolishly lost the relationship with his son, daughter-in-law, and their children for over 20 years and died an angry, unforgiving man. It was such an unfortunate conclusion to something that could have been so different had he sought help from the Lord, practiced forgiveness, laid aside his grievances, confessed his stubbornness, and applied biblical principles to his relationship with their daughter-in-law. If Jerry had tried, their relationship lights would probably have all come back on. The situation may have remained stressful, but it would have been so much better than having no relationship at all!

This should serve as a warning if you can't or won't control your emotions. Words, like bullets, are hard to retract once they're fired at another person. Uncontrolled anger and its consequences have been illustrated for us throughout the Scriptures. Saul in the Old Testament became very angry with David to the extent that he tried numerous times to kill him (see 1 Samuel 19–24). Nabal was a fool and, because of his words, nearly destroyed his household (1 Samuel 25). Absalom became angry with his father David. He also tried to take over David's leadership and kingdom through lies and threats (2 Samuel 15). Many other examples serve as reminders to us of the danger of "blowing a fuse" or "burning a circuit" in uncontrolled anger.

Maybe you have your own issues with anger and can remember "losing your cool" and doing damage to your family or relationships with friends or employers. Many who come to my office for counseling are filled with uncontrolled anger or rage for one reason or another. What we refer to today as "road rage" is nothing more than another display of uncontrolled anger or blown fuse. Check any of the latest news events, and anger is generally the root cause of problems like child abuse, murders, terror attacks, and family conflict. In our story at the beginning of this section, Tony finally "blew a fuse" with Jessie, and we see him, other siblings, and parents suffering as a result.

Over and over again the Bible warns against allowing your emotions to get the best of you, resulting in angry outbursts. Ponder some of these verses and draw your own conclusions.

A quick-tempered man acts foolishly, and a man of evil devices is hated. (Proverbs 14:17)

It is better to live in a desert land than with a contentious and vexing woman. (Proverbs 21:19)

Do not associate with a man given to anger; or go with a hot-tempered man, or you will learn his ways and find a snare for yourself. (Proverbs 22:24–25)

The north wind brings forth rain, and a backbiting tongue, an angry countenance. (Proverbs 25:23)

An angry man stirs up strife, and a hot-tempered man abounds in transgression. (Proverbs 29:22)

Do not be eager in your heart to be angry, for anger resides in the bosom of fools. (Ecclesiastes 7:9)

Everyone must be quick to hear, slow to speak and slow to anger; for the anger of man does not achieve the righteousness of God. (James 1:19–20)

Parents, please remember that uncontrolled anger, malicious speech, angry thoughts, and angry behavior toward your toxic son- or daughter-in-law will eventually leave you in a dark and lonely place, separating you from your son or daughter and grandchildren. The same is true for siblings with a toxic brother- or sister-in-law. Anger and rage will destroy your relationship with that person, and will also destroy your Christian testimony. Trust me, the toxic person in your life will eventually succeed in breaking your family apart *unless* you control your temper and practice biblical principles of Christlike behavior. Blowing a fuse will only result in family heartache and a severe "power outage" in your home and family relationships.

CHAPTER
TWENTY-ONE

Taming the Tongue

What gets parents (or in Tony's case, siblings) in the most trouble happens when they open their mouths. The tongue is very powerful. As we see in Proverbs, it has the power of life and death (Proverbs 18:21). When we "blow a fuse" or an emotional circuit, this most often results in a torrent of angry, hurtful words.

But even when your words aren't spoken in anger or with spite, with a toxic in-law, what we say is almost always interpreted as an intrusion, criticism, or unnecessary. It might seem to your married children that you're asserting your parental authority, or that you are assuming they can't make their own decisions or that they will make the wrong decisions.

Be careful about this. Guard your words carefully and watch how you say things. Once careless words fly off your tongue, they are like a bullet speeding out the end of a rifle. You can't stop them, and you can't easily repair the damage they cause.

Here are some insights from the Bible regarding our speech:

1. **When you speak, consider how your words will be received.** A careless tongue drives people away or makes them bite back. "A gentle answer turns away wrath, but a harsh word stirs up anger" (Proverbs 15:1); "the mouth of fools spouts folly" (Proverbs 15:2); "a soothing tongue is a tree of life, but perversion in it crushes the spirit" (Proverbs 15:4).

2. **Be quick to hear and slow to speak.** Nearly everyone is familiar with this verse: "Everyone must be quick to hear, slow to speak and slow to anger; for the anger of man does not achieve the righteousness of God" (James 1:19–20). It seems to me the old adage "God gave you one mouth and two ears, and they should be used proportionately" should be carefully applied.

3. **Don't ignore the damage the tongue can cause.** James 3:2 reminds us that "we all stumble in many ways. If anyone does not stumble in what he says, he is a perfect man, able to bridle the whole body as well." He goes on to say, "The tongue is a small part of the body, and yet it boasts of great things…. the tongue is set among our members as that which defiles the entire body … no one can tame the tongue; it is a restless evil and full of deadly poison. With it we bless our Lord and Father, and with it we curse men… My brethren, these things ought not to be this way" (James 3:5–10).

4. **Read Proverbs to learn more about controlling the tongue**
   Occasionally for our daily devotions, my wife and I read
   a chapter in Proverbs following the calendar day. For example
   on the 10th of any given month, we read Proverbs 10. I'm
   shocked at how much Proverbs says about our speech and the
   foolishness of disgruntled, cantankerous, and frustrated people
   Watch your speech and avoid conflicts with your sometimes
   foolish son- or daughter-in-law.

How many parents have damaged relationships because they
can't keep their mouths shut? Those parents live under the
impression that everyone cares about what they think. They
assume falsely that their son- or daughter-in-law can't wait
to hear their exhaustive diatribe on how they should live their
lives. It just doesn't work like that, even if your family members
aren't particularly toxic or difficult!

If you're asked for your opinion, present it as an option
not the obvious right answer. For example, should your child
or son- or daughter-in-law ask you about a parenting matter
it seems safer to answer, "Here is my opinion, but I trust your
judgment and will support whatever you decide."

We would all do well to remember that old saying, "It's better
to keep your mouth shut and have everyone think you're a fool
than to open it and prove everyone right." Learn to smile a lot
keep your mouth shut and pray.

CHAPTER TWENTY-TWO

Loving the Difficult

One evening some years back, I was walking to the barn to milk cows when I noticed a baby raccoon growling at me from inside a small culvert. The little creature was scared, mad, and not about to come out of the pipe. He was probably orphaned and trying to make it on his own. Being the crazy cowboy that I am, I decided to catch the little critter—hopefully without losing a finger in the process.

I put my milk bucket on one end of the culvert to block the little raccoon's exit. Then I placed a few other boards at the other end to close off his other escape route. After making sure my new friend couldn't go anywhere, I ran to the barn to get a bigger bucket and a piece of plywood for my final move. I figured if I opened one end of the culvert and stuck the handle of a pitchfork into it, he'd naturally go out the opposite end. This proved a good strategy, and within the hour out he came. He didn't know I was lying on top of the pipe, bucket in hand, waiting for his exit. As soon as he came out, down banged the bucket, trapping the little guy inside. Boy, was he mad now! I slid the piece of plywood under the bucket so when I turned the bucket over, the wood served as the lid. Smart, right?

My next problem was figuring out what to do with the angry little raccoon I'd caught. Releasing him into the feed room seemed as good a place as anywhere else. So that's what I did, and the little guy spent his first night in my feed room.

The next morning, we both got a good look at each other. His bared teeth and ferocious growl indicated he was a very unhappy camper. But I loved his fluffy long tail and beautiful eyes. With increasing courage (or maybe stupidity), I reached out to pet his little, angry head.

I felt his bite through my double-layered leather gloves. But rather than focusing on his nasty disposition, sharp teeth, and intimidating growl, I decided to focus on his beautiful tail, his cute little ears, and his bright eyes. I paid no attention to his other negative attributes. I told myself I was more determined, bigger, and smarter than he was. I gave him some leftover sausages, pork chop bones, and pieces of ribeye steak to tempt him. Those delicacies got his attention, and our friendship started to blossom.

Eventually, the little squirt would meet me at the grain room door, climb up on my shoulder, eat out of my hand, and sleep in my lap. He was the cutest friend an old cowboy could have. I concluded something from this experience. Life goes a lot better when you focus on the good things rather than the bad. While my little friend was pretty difficult and had a bad disposition at first, I ignored those things and focused on his good qualities. And our relationship eventually improved significantly. It was hard for me to release him into the wild some time later.

No matter who you are or where you work, you'll run into difficult people. Difficult people can be like my little raccoon friend—they growl and bite and are tough to deal with. When you're faced with such a person, the question becomes how to best work with that person. If you work with them at your job it's one thing. If you go to church with them, it can present a challenge but it's workable. However, if your son or daughter marries a difficult person, that's quite a different matter. At work you can quit, transfer, write them up, fire them, or ignore them, get your work done, and go home. At church, you can have moments of kindness and maybe some fellowship.

However, if a difficult person becomes a part of your family, you are faced with the situation day in and day out, month in and month out, year in and year out. You can't transfer to another family, you can't fire the person, and you can't ignore the problem. Well, you could, but it's not necessarily the spiritual, Christlike solution. First Corinthians 12:31–13:8 shows us a "more excellent way."

I'm sure you're familiar with 1 Corinthians 13, the great exposition on love. But let's look just a bit more carefully at each of the fifteen definitions of love. The first two in the list are positive qualities, and the following eight are negative descriptions representing a lack of love. The final grouping points to the lasting nature of love.

- **Love is patient and kind.** Both of these are great virtues and express the selfless servanthood of the Christian father- and mother-in-law. In spite of the unacceptable behavior of a difficult son- or daughter-in-law they continue to be patient, suffer long, and remain kind.

- **Love is not jealous, bragging, or arrogant.** These three monsters terrorize people with the spirit of self-righteousness and self-centeredness. "I'm better than you" is a common response from difficult people, but it's not the way of love. "I'm jealous of who you are" again encapsulates the heart of a difficult person's selfishness but isn't a life of love.

- **Love doesn't act unbecomingly or seek its own. Love isn't easily provoked to anger.** On the other hand, love acts properly, even when mistreated, always thinks of others first, keeps anger under control, and forgives voluntarily. James 4:1–2 says it all: "What is the source of quarrels and conflicts among you? Is not the source your pleasures that wage war in your members? You lust and do not have; so you commit murder. You are envious and cannot obtain; so you fight and quarrel." Love doesn't seek its own and isn't easily provoked to anger.

- **Love finds no joy in unrighteousness but rejoices in the truth.** Unrighteous attitudes and behavior are never acceptable to the person who loves. Rather love finds strength in the truth.

- **Love bears all things, believes all things, hopes all things, endures all things. Love never fails.** When plans fail and life dishes out disappointment, be assured that there's one spiritual characteristic that you can always count on. Love will always bring blessing, right to the very end.

The conclusion of this section might be this. Allow love to overlook the negative character flaws in your difficult son- or daughter-in-law (or in Tony's case, your difficult sister-in-law). Be forgiving and focus on areas of their character or interests that are helpful. Be an encourager to them in those areas.

Let's think back to our story of Jessie, Max, and Tony. Jessie was very artistic and an excellent interior decorator. She did a fantastic job at making her home look terrific. She loved to play with colors and trim that accentuated their modest home. On the occasions when Max and Jessie came to my office for counseling, she was always dressed in the most modern attire. She loved to be creative with her style and the atest fashion. Breaking into Jessie's unpleasant personality might be as simple as taking an interest in her artistic skills or asking her to update your bathroom accessories and remodel your workout room. This could work wonders for Tony or one of the other sibling's relationship with her.

Although Jessie's character leaves much to be desired (especially her anger issues), she is extraordinarily gifted at helping people. She could easily help someone with their finances, insurance matters, or vacation planning. Encouraging her to explore her giftedness might just remove some tension in the relationship. Connecting her with friends or other church members could be encouraging too. All of this could make a difficult woman feel appreciated by her in-laws.

The idea is to look for areas you can use as positive building blocks to validate your toxic son- or daughter-in-law and build a workable relationship with him or her. Maybe your difficult son-in-law likes playing video games. Try asking him to teach you how to play. That sounds easy, but it really isn't. If he's interested in hunting and fishing, that would be easier for me—I can just be myself! Learn about his interests. Maybe you could buy him a new fishing rod or other kind of equipment he would use. Whatever it is, keep your anger in check, keep your tongue under control, and look for the positive qualities you can encourage or areas where you can show interest. You may find the snarling, teeth-baring raccoon ends up becoming your friend.

Part Six
Problematic Christians

CHAPTER
TWENTY-THREE

"Christian" Extremists

I need to remind you that this book isn't about toxic fathers-or mothers-in-law but rather sons- and daughters-in-law who are detrimental to family unity and fellowship for a number of reasons. The most dangerous and hurtful sons- and daughters-in-law are those who profess to be Christians but bring emotional pain, separation, shunning, indifference, and self-righteousness into the home of their fathers- and mothers-in-law. Read the following story and you'll see what I'm talking about.

Steve and Alyssa wanted to see their daughter Ann pursue a Christian college experience. They felt a Bible school would be a safe place for Ann to study, and she agreed. So, in the fall, Ann headed off to a Christian college in the Midwest. It was there she met Dan. During their college experience Dan and Ann fell in love, and they married shortly after graduation.

It wasn't long into their marriage that Dan's unbiblical, legalistic, and frightening doctrines began to surface. Dan, his parents, and their church believed that they were "blameless" (i.e., without sin) and demanded from their constituency what they called "unity in all truth." This meant everyone had to agree with all of their biblical interpretations or suffer church discipline and shunning. Dan's paranoid and power-hungry father was pastor of their home church of approximately 25 people.

Much pressure was put on Steve and Alyssa to unilaterally agree with the false teachings of Dan's family's church. In response, Steve discussed with Dan and his parents the issues of "blamelessness" and "unity in all truth." Steve was a good Bible student in his own right, so he knew what he was talking about when it came to the Bible.

However, what began with the best intentions on Steve's part ended in disaster. Dan and his pastor-father couldn't tolerate that Steve did not agree with them. Moreover, it became clear that they lacked the ability to carry on a discussion without feeling threatened or intimidated and becoming hostile. So, despite Steve's gentle and thoughtful interaction, Dan, Ann, Dan's parents and their church brought Steve and Alyssa under church discipline (even though they weren't actually part of the church) and shunned them from any contact with Ann, their own daughter. Furthermore, they demanded that Ann have no relationship with her parents until Steve and Alyssa repented of their "errors" and chose to agree with the church's teachings.

That was 10 years ago. Since then, Dan and Ann have refused to have any contact with her parents. They have since had three children, all of whom Steve and Alyssa have never seen except through pictures secured by friends. Steve and Alyssa are not allowed to have any contact with their grandchildren. Dan and Ann even returned Christmas and birthday gifts sent for the grandchildren. (Just a side note: other leading families in Dan's church have shunned their family members as well. Steve and Alyssa aren't the only family hurt by this cult.)

You might think this description of Dan, his parents, and their church is harsh and exaggerated. But let me assure you that it isn't. Not only are members required to shun anyone who disagrees with them, part of their teaching involves beating infants as young as 2 months old with a wooden stick for making noises during church services. If you didn't punish your babies as instructed, you would be shunned. Thankfully, due to the involvement of concerned and courageous friends, this fact was brought to the police, who brought charges against several people in the church for child abuse and conspiracy to commit child abuse. Several people were found guilty in the court of law and received stiff sentencing.

This is just one family out of many that I have counseled in which a so-called Christian has ignored biblical teaching on the value of unity, peace, and fellowship in God's family. It's safe to say that such behavior has severely damaged many godly families. Furthermore, these individuals have brought shame and disgrace to the name of Christ through their self-righteousness, unbridled legalism, and disdain for other Christians with whom they don't or won't "agree to disagree."

The Book of Proverbs speaks to people such as Dan and his parents:

> Doing wickedness is like sport to a fool. (Proverbs 10:23)

> The way of a fool is right in his own eyes, but a wise man is he who listens to counsel. (Proverbs 12:15)

> A fool is arrogant and careless. A quick-tempered man acts foolishly. (Proverbs 14:16, 17)

> Let a man meet a bear robbed of her cubs, rather than a fool in his folly. (Proverbs 17:12)

> A fool does not delight in understanding, but only in revealing his own mind. (Proverbs 18:2)

> Do not speak in the hearing of a fool, for he will despise the wisdom of your words. (Proverbs 23:9)

I think you get the picture. Dan and his parents fall into the category of these proverbial fools. Their egotistical attitudes, power-hungry doctrines, and emotional insecurity have brought great damage to many families, especially to Steve and Alyssa's.

Unbiblical Christian extremists don't just hurt family relationships, they destroy the testimony of the Church of Jesus Christ, His Bride (Ephesians 5:23–27), through their destructive shunning and abusive practices. I have learned that these toxic, so-called Christian sons- or daughters-in-law like to use the Bible not for personal sanctification but as a club to bash the heads of others. Somehow, they can find all sorts of reasons to justify their meanness and dis-fellowshipping or shunning of others, but they never get to the passages on making peace, preserving unity, loving others, serving others, encouraging others, and being merciful to those with whom you disagree.

I hope you never have to deal with such a person, but I know many families that have to interact with this kind of individual regularly. So let's look at some pointers for dealing with such a person.

CHAPTER TWENTY-FOUR

Agree to Disagree

Let's think for a minute about how this situation with Dan and Ann could have possibly been avoided. First and foremost, let me say that I don't blame Steve or Alyssa for discussing doctrines with Dan and his parents. They couldn't possibly expect such extreme and abusive actions from people who profess to be reasonable Christians. In this particular case, they opened a "hornet's nest."

My counsel to parents is to be very careful of entering into difficult discussions with a toxic son- or daughter-in-law, lest you end up in a very unhealthy place. A toxic, controlling, highly opinionated, insecure, easily intimidated son- or daughter-in-law is not the type of person who handles differences of opinion or conflict very well. They don't like to be confronted, advised or offered guidance. They want to be in charge over everyone, including your son or daughter, and even you. My advice is this: be careful, keep your mouth shut, smile a lot and pray. Is that starting to sound familiar? I know I might be sounding like a broken record, but it's the best advice I can give. It's better to let the Holy Spirit go to work in these hard situations.

When you do address differences of opinions with your adult child or your in-law, take great care and tread very cautiously. I've found it's best to approach such subjects or situations with more questions than answers. Dialogue is always better than monologue. Learn to be more interested in the opinions and conclusions of others by asking questions that begin with how, why, where, when, and to what degree. Come with an attitude of being a seeker or learner, rather than someone who is authoritative, has all the answers, or is always right. A humble attitude will take the heat out of the disagreement. (We'll talk more about humility in the next chapter.)

Here is another important thing to remember: many sons and daughters look at their parents as if they're some relic from the far distant past, like dinosaurs. I can assure you, your sons- and daughters-in-law (even those who aren't toxic or difficult) have the same outlook. Dad's and Mom's wisdom, though based on years of experience, doesn't seem to hold water for the new generation. The world you grew up in is so different from theirs!

That last statement is certainly true. Change is part of life. The world we live in is changing constantly. So many things in our society are very different from when I was a young person. Technology has changed so many things, and so have our societal perceptions (definitely not all for the better).

People's commitment to marriage has changed. Attitudes toward divorce have changed. The feminist movement has brought change to family roles and attitudes. Parenting has changed too.

I bring this up because it's important to remember this when trying to help your son or daughter and their spouse live life more skillfully and more wisely. As a parent, great care must be given to this challenging process. You need to realize that your child and their spouse probably have a different understanding of what it means to "live more skillfully and more wisely" in the 21st century.

When you do give advice, I'd always communicate my thoughts as just an "opinion," or an "option," or an "alternative" to be mixed with their spouse's thoughts or others views on the subject. I'd always leave room for my son- or daughter-in-law to do what they think best, even though my opinion might be different. If my grandson is outside in the snow without boots, I might say, "Would you like for me to put boots on Billy, or is he having a learning experience?" If it's okay with Billy's dad and mom, it's okay with me. Doctors at the emergency room who treat frostbitten toes have much more authority than Grandpa and Grandma.

When should you give your advice or opinion? I would suggest only when it's invited. If your daughter-in-law asks you how to properly cook a pizza or place the dishes in the dishwasher, then I think you could offer some help.

If your son-in-law asks you to help him fix the lawnmower, then give him a hand. Don't do it for him but work with him. But if your son or daughter and their spouse want new carpet and don't ask for your opinion, parents should be okay with that. When it comes to parenting, younger generations have different ideas about discipline, food, sleeping, toys, babysitters, and you name it. So grandparents, tread carefully! Remember, it's usually best just to smile, keep your mouth shut and pray.

However—and this is a big "however"—if someone's physical safety is at risk, I would call this to their attention. For example, if Daddy lets little Billy play with his loaded pistol, I'd say something or do something. In Steve and Alyssa's story, someone noted the abusive practices of Dan and his family's church and reported them to the police. I believe that was the right thing to do.

Look at it this way. Absolute biblical principles and issues of safety need support and protection. Let me give you an example. Many years ago, my friend Gary had a son-in-law, Bob. They got into a discussion about alcohol consumption. Bob was (and is) a very legalistic person, almost to the point of believing in a "works-based" salvation. This led to a rather pointed discussion which Bob didn't handle very well. When Gary didn't totally agree with him, Bob's anger accelerated and it changed the entire course of their relationship. Bob's frustration with Gary caused Bob to become more distant, more isolated, and more controlling of Gary's daughter, Barb.

Over time, Bob refused to allow Gary to hug or be affectionate with Barb. He wouldn't allow them time alone—even when Bob went to the bathroom, she had to go with him! I know, it sounds really weird and controlling, doesn't it? When Gary's father died, Bob allowed Barb to stay with Gary and her mother for the memorial service, but she had to keep notes on all their interactions and report back to him. He did everything possible to cut off Barb from her parents, but Gary and his wife persevered, practicing these biblical principles. As you might expect, Barb's marriage to Bob eventually ended in a divorce.

There are times when we must consider addressing difficult issues like biblical doctrines and physically, emotionally, or spiritually abusive behavior. Such was the situation in which Steve and Alyssa found themselves. If Steve didn't broach the subject, no one would. And referring Dan and Ann to another outside resource like a mentor, a different pastor, or a biblical counselor was out of the question because of Dan's father's relentless control and know-it-all attitude.

Under the best of conditions, confronting such issues is very dangerous territory with extreme consequences if we're not careful. So be very cautious in how you approach the confrontation. Display an attitude of being a seeker or learner rather than being authoritative and right all the time. Strive for dialogue, not debate. Debate generally forces people into the corner or puts them in the defensive mode of defending positions and resisting change, whereas dialogue searches for options and other opinions, paving the way to new possibilities. The conversation (and your relationship with that person) will go more smoothly if you focus on dialogue instead of debate.

In less severe cases, methodology (how people chose to do things) is open to a wide variety of application and action. There is enormous freedom to do things in different ways depending on personality, interest, and capability. For example, let's say your son-in-law doesn't know a thing about painting the baby's new nursery. Your daughter doesn't mind him learning on the job by doing it together. Great! Stay out of the way, compliment the finished paint job and have a soda. They may not want your opinion, so just keep your thoughts to yourself and smile a lot. Maybe the church they decided to attend isn't consistent with your opinion. Or, they have unsaved friends you don't think are a good influence. Or their parenting isn't like what yours used to be. So what? Smile, keep your mouth shut, and pray.

This may seem more like human wisdom than biblical wisdom, but the Bible does encourage us to be mindful of others and "regard one another as more important than yourselves; do not merely look out for your own personal interests, but also for the interests of others" (Philippians 2:3–4). This might include learning about the other person's opinions, expectations, and goals, and the process for accomplishing them.

And above all, remember that you are trying to protect and preserve the relationship—with your son- or daughter-in-law, but especially the one with your adult child. I've learned the importance of this from many parents. It's not easy, but it is absolutely necessary. My advice is, once again, smile a lot keep your mouth shut and pray lest you lose relationship with your son or daughter. Agree to disagree.

Keep in mind the verses from Scripture on unity and humility, especially when dealing with disagreement or differences in opinion. You might want to hit your difficult son- or daughter-in-law over the head with these (and they probably would deserve it). But these verses are crucial for parents to remember too because parents can also be very strong-willed, stubborn, and authoritative. They can forget the teaching of Galatians 5:22—23 on the "fruit of the Spirit' and fail to apply this fruit and the teachings of Scripture to difficult relationships. (This is especially easy to do if you are in a heated debate or intense argument.) So learn these verses and ponder them before you enter any kind of discussion with your child or in-law.

> How good and how pleasant it is for brothers to dwell together in unity! (Psalm 133:1)

Finally, brethren, rejoice, be made complete, be comforted, be like-minded, live in peace. (2 Corinthians 13:11)

Beyond all these things put on love, which is the perfect bond of unity. Let the peace of Christ rule in your hearts. (Colossians 3:14–15)

And the seed whose fruit is righteousness is sown in peace by those who make peace. (James 3:18)

CHAPTER
TWENTY–FIVE

Humility – The Equalizer

Thus says the Lord, "Let not a wise man boast of his wisdom, and let not the mighty man boast of his might, let not a rich man boast of his riches; but let him who boasts boast of this, that he understands and knows Me, that I am the Lord who exercises lovingkindness, justice and righteousness on earth; for I delight in these things," declares the Lord. (Jeremiah 9:23)

In the last chapter, I mentioned the importance of humility when entering into any kind of discussion with your adult child and their spouse. Let me tell you a story that illustrates exactly how crucial humility is to these kinds of heated (or potentially heated) family situations.

George and Sandy are full-time workers for a parachurch organization that promotes evangelism around the world. But they live in the good old USA and minister to churches and retiring missionaries. They raised two daughters, both of whom are married and living in different states.

Their daughter Sally married Mark, a pastor of a small country church. Jean, their other daughter, also married a Christian man, named Bill.

Not too long ago, George and Sandy found themselves caught in the middle of a dispute between their adult children. This happens in many families, even though adult children should know better. Of course, Dad and Mom are generally stuck in the middle, struggling with what to do and how to go about keeping peace among those they love. Sally and Jean had a quarrel over how much time George and Sandy spend with each family and about the way Jean and Bill parent. Things were said between the sisters that were hurtful, and they entered the "no talking," "no contact" zone, even though they are both Christians who should know better.

But what made the situation even worse was that Sally's husband Mark stepped in and cut off any contact between his family and Jean and Bill. On top of that, Mark told Sally to cut off contact with her parents too, because he believed George and Sandy were not punishing Jean and Bill for their unkind and sinful words. Furthermore, he refused to allow George and Sandy access to their grandchildren (Mark and Sally's kids) until they took a stand against Jean and Bill by cutting off all communication with them.

What a pickle this family was in when George and Sandy were referred to me for counseling! They didn't know what to do and needed help on how to manage this horrible situation.

George and Sandy, in essence, were victims of Mark, who was acting like a toxic son-in-law, with his controlling and legalistic beliefs and his lack of biblical perspective and Christlike humility. Blaming and punishing everyone else because he believed he and Sally were treated wrongly was no help to anybody. Mark and Sally were trying to coerce George and Sandy into acting according to their wishes by refusing to allow them visits with their grandchildren. This was more arrogance and pride, especially for people claiming to be followers of Christ! Where was their humility?

When I met with George and Sandy, I could sense their painful emotions building up and turning their spiritual convictions upside down. Anger, frustration, hurt, anxiety, fear, and many other emotions were starting to surface and making matters so much worse. Their spiritual "pipeline" needed to be cleaned out, getting rid of all the unbiblical thoughts, so that God's Word and grace could flow through them. A humble heart and attitude are essential to keeping our spiritual pipelines free of gunk so that the fruit of the Spirit—love, joy, peace, patience, kindness, goodness, faithfulness, gentleness, and self-control—can flow freely (Galatians 5:22–23).

Let's remind ourselves of the importance of humility from a biblical perspective. The Christlike character undergirding the fruit of the Spirit is a lifestyle built upon biblical humility. George and Sandy certainly found this to be a prerequisite in their family struggles. The sinful pride of their son-in-law Mark, if met in kind with sinful pride from George and Sandy, would have created a firestorm of negative, irreconcilable emotions, words, and damage.

Read carefully with me this passage from Philippians 2:5–9:

> Have this attitude in yourselves which was also in Christ Jesus, who, although He existed in the form of God, did not regard equality with God a thing to be grasped, but emptied Himself, taking the form of a bond-servant, and being made in the likeness of men. Being found in appearance as a man, He *humbled* Himself by becoming obedient to the point of death, even death on a cross. For this reason also, God highly exalted Him, and bestowed on Him the name which is above every name. (italics added)

If God's people would put this passage into practice in their personal lives, many hurtful situations would be resolved. We would think the way Christ does and set aside our lofty expectations, overly sensitive tendencies, and high-mindedness. If humility replaced stubbornness, we would all have servants' hearts eager and willing to serve others before ourselves.

When a spirit of pride replaces a spirit of humility, relational troubles are inevitable. You see, pride produces the attitude of "my way or the highway." Pride demands control over a situation and over others. It reveals itself in pushy, self-righteous, critical attitudes. Pride will try to manipulate through fear, obligation, and guilt. (Remember FOG from Chapter 9?) And if pride doesn't get its own way, it will have a huge pity party.

The Bible has a lot to say about humility. Humility was one of God's conditions for Israel's healing:

> "If … My people who are called by My name humble themselves and pray and seek My face and turn from their wicked ways, then I will hear from heaven, will forgive their sin and will heal their land." (2 Chronicles 7:13–14)

God required humility from Israel, along with prayer, a longing for relationship with God, and repentance. I think it's safe to say that these four attributes will go a long way in mending relationships with other people too.

When you're tempted to act and speak in a prideful way, remember this from Proverbs: "A man's pride will bring him low, but a humble spirit will obtain honor" (Proverbs 29:23). Wouldn't you rather be honored than brought low? The apostle Paul exhorts us to "put on . . . humility" in Colossians 3:12. Paul isn't making a suggestion; rather he is giving Christians a command.

The apostle Peter echoes Paul's words when he instructs us to "clothe yourselves with humility toward one another, for God is opposed to the proud, but gives grace to the humble." (1 Peter 5:5). Peter himself had to learn some pretty hard lessons during his adventures with Jesus. But learn them he did, and he instructs us to be humble. A humble spirit before God will lead to a humble attitude, and humble actions toward others, even toward difficult people like toxic in-laws.

This would be the message to you from our friends George and Sandy: be humble. Their humble attitudes enabled them to build bridges to toxic Mark and Sally, restoring their relationship and renewing grandparent visits. Yes, it took an extended period of time, but patient perseverance paid great dividends. Their two daughters are now reconciled, and the whole family gets together for various outings and holidays. This is a real victory of reconciliation.

When a spirit of pride replaces a spirit of humility,
relational troubles are inevitable.

CHAPTER TWENTY-SIX

Matters of Church Discipline

Since the concept of church discipline came up in Steve and Alyssa's story, I want to briefly address the subject here Church discipline of a son or daughter, or son- or daughter-in-law is one of the most difficult situations a parent can face.

Often in my family ministry I've needed to face a church discipline matter. I'll give you an example. Let's say that your son or son-in-law gets involved in an adulterous affair After much counsel and help from their church family he remains unrepentant. There might even be a marital separation in process and/or divorce proceedings. Let's assume that the church elders have decided to publicly discipline your son or son-in-law and put him out of fellowship after following the teaching in Matthew 18:15-17. What are you to do?

What would that mean for your family relationships to have a family member put out of fellowship by the church?

I understand the biblical principles concerning church discipline as taught in Matthew 18:15–17 and 1 Corinthians 5:9–13. The result of such church discipline is summarized as "let him be to you as a Gentile and a tax collector" (Matthew 18:17) or "not to associate with any so-called brother if he is an immoral person" (1 Corinthians 5:11). God instituted the church discipline process to protect his church family from internal decay.

But does this church discipline extend to family relationships including children, spouses, and extended family members of the person who is under the discipline? If a woman's husband comes under church discipline, does that mean she should "not associate with" him? Does it mean that a disciplined father should be treated as a Gentile and a tax collector" by his children? Would church discipline extend to a father and mother of a son or daughter or their spouse who's under church discipline? Should the parents have nothing to do with their adult child or in-law who's under church discipline? These are very difficult questions.

Do you think God intended that church discipline should fracture family relationships as well?

Let me give you an example of an all-too-common scenario. About 3 years ago, I counseled with Shelly, a wife and mom of five who was under church discipline from an extremist church. Shelly's husband had complained to the pastor that she wanted to attend a different church. The pastor counseled him to leave Shelly, and she was subsequently excommunicated by the church. Shelly was abandoned by her husband and left alone to care for the kids, all because she had a different opinion on which church the family should attend! As I write Shelly and her husband are still separated, and he lives with the pastor who supported and encouraged his outrageous behavior.

Carrying over church discipline into family relationships creates all kinds of havoc. It results in men and women excommunicating or shunning spouses, children, parents aunts, uncles, siblings, in-laws, and may even include the family pets. What a mess! It's my belief, from Bible teachings on family relationships, that church discipline should remain just that: church discipline. It belongs in a church context and should not cross over into the extended family context.

The New Testament speaks directly to family issues (love of husband for wife, subjection of wife to husband, obedience of children to parents; see Ephesians 5:25–6:4) in many places, but it never advocates the excommunication of family members. That isn't to say that some problems within a family can be very serious and scandalous and may need some type of intervention. But using a form of "church discipline" to justify abandoning a family member is unacceptable. That's the type of thing the Pharisees in Jesus' day would have done The religious elite of Jesus' day advocated divorce for any reason because of the hardness of their hearts (Mark 10:5). Jesus brought clarity to the subject (in Matthew 5:32) teaching that divorce was only permissible in the case of adultery. There's something very special and precious about the family unit, and I believe God seeks to protect the family unit through relational responsibilities that continue even in the midst of sin and disagreements, which happen in every family.

I'll summarize briefly some of these relational responsibilities.

- **Husbands**: You are to sacrificially love your wife as Christ loves the church (Ephesians 5:25), understand and honor her (1 Peter 3:7), love her as you love yourself (Ephesians 5:33), and provide for her (1 Timothy 5:8).

- **Wives**: You are to respect and reverence your husband (Ephesians 5:33), be his helper (Genesis 2:18), and follow his leadership (Ephesians 5:24).

- **Parents**: You are to raise your children under the instruction and guidance of the Lord (Ephesians 6:4) and not provoke them to anger by being harsh, impatient, or abusive (Ephesians 6:4).

- **Children**: You are to obey your parents while showing them honor and respect (Ephesians 6:1–2).

Church discipline doesn't abrogate these fundamental family responsibilities. Sin must be dealt with in the context of the family unit. We must all strive to confess, ask forgiveness, and repent of hurtful behavior so that the family unit remains together and effective in applying biblical principles.

It's my belief, from Bible teachings on family relationships, that church discipline should remain just that: church discipline.

Part Seven
Branches on the Vine

CHAPTER
TWENTY-SEVEN

Clinging to the Vine

Well, we've been through a lot together in this book. We've heard a number of sad, depressing stories about toxic sons- and daughters-in law. And we've looked at what it means to live the Christian life in these situations. Out of all the biblical principles, strategies, and examples we've discussed, John 15:1–5 gives us the fundamental answer to how we can live that life. We who are the branches must draw life-giving strength and nourishment from the Vine which is Christ. Without Him, we can do nothing. Attempting to live the Christian life on our own, especially in difficult situations, is a futile exercise in religious practice. Through the Vine, the Holy Spirit enables and empowers us to live a Christlike lifestyle, obedient to the teachings of Scripture. We need the Vine!

Before we end, I'd like to introduce you to one more family who has suffered tremendously under the influence of a highly toxic son-in-law. Let me give you some background before we start on Jim and Wendy's story. I first met with Jim and Wendy to counsel them about issues related to their daughter Linda. They were having serious difficulties with some of her decisions, especially those related to her then-boyfriend. A few years after our initial counseling sessions, Jim had a medical event and died unexpectedly. Now a widow, Wendy was left not only with the responsibility of maintaining their eight other children, which she did faithfully, but also with a turbulent situation brought on by a toxic son-in-law.

I will warn you, it's a gut-wrenching story, but in it, you'll see Wendy's deep faith and perseverance in the midst of such life-shattering tragedy. Delight in God's work in Wendy's life as Christ the Vinedresser nurtures, sustains, and comforts her. Be encouraged in your own struggles as Wendy moves closer to Jesus Christ and becomes much more fruitful, drawing incredible strength from the Vine.

The last few years have been extremely challenging, but I have seen the Lord work in my life, and He has shown Himself to be faithful to me and my family. Trusting God takes courage as He allows trying circumstances to come my way. But in the midst of it all, I've grown to trust Him more and lean solely on Him. That's a slight exaggeration because, as you will learn, I still struggle with my negative emotions, sometimes bitterness, discouragement, and resentment. It's true, confession is good for the soul.

Actually, both Jim and I were making great progress after talking with you. That is, until Jim passed away and I felt the loss, loneliness, and mounting responsibilities. I felt the full weight of being a single parent to nine children and struggled to find courage to persevere.

As you know, it was with our daughter Linda that we needed wisdom and perspective. Linda was always our fun-loving and creative girl. She had an endless supply of energy for organizing group activities and spent much of her time volunteering at our church camp. Linda was also our strong-willed child and went through a couple years of rebellion. It was at this time we fasted and prayed continually for God to do something in her life.

After a couple of years of college, she came home and enrolled in a local school for a few classes. It was at this school that she met Baxter. They dated for a very short time before getting serious.

One of our first encounters with Baxter was when Linda asked Jim to pick him up from work. Baxter had lost his driver's license due to a reckless driving citation. We were a bit taken aback to discover that Baxter lived with his parents in a filthy apartment in a very seedy neighborhood. We all went out to lunch. That was interesting to say the least. Afterward, when Jim and I were alone, we concluded that we'd never met such an arrogant, know-it-all kid. Instantly we became incredibly worried about this relationship.

I distinctly remember the Thanksgiving Day when Linda came home and announced that she and Baxter were going to get married in the next few weeks. It was unbelievable! We tried to encourage her to take some time and reevaluate her decision. After all, they hadn't been a couple that long. I so wanted her to wait a while. She became very angry with him and me as a result of our words of caution and lack of affirmation. After that, Linda's calls and visits to our home became infrequent at best. She and Baxter continued to date. What compounded the problem was Linda had moved out of our home and our communication with her had already become minimal.

Why don't Jim and Wendy end Linda's relationship with Baxter? Can they do that?

When we were able to talk to Linda and Baxter, we encouraged them to go through premarital counseling and pleaded with Linda to introduce Baxter to her friends to get their feedback. Baxter had isolated her from friends and family, saying, "You only need me for your happiness." It was during this time that Jim and I came to get advice from you on how to handle this situation. I distinctly remember you advising us that, no matter what, we needed to maintain a line of communication with Linda, refuse to let Baxter ruin our relationship with her, and be careful to not burn bridges we later may have to cross. We kept trying to talk to her, telling her we loved her, and inviting them to meals at our home.

What was driving Linda to make such a hasty decision?

If Baxter was a God-honoring believer, how should he have responded to the rift between Linda and her parents?

It was with a final statement of rebellion that Linda and Baxter eventually got married. Linda said to me one day "You will never want me to marry Baxter, so I am going to do it anyway." Their wedding was incredibly awkward and hurtful to us. We gave them money to go somewhere nice for their wedding night, but instead Baxter took Linda back to his parents' apartment to sleep on the floor. What a pathetic way to start off their life together.

How should Jim and Wendy try to establish a better relationship with Baxter? Take into consideration what Proverbs 9:7—8 says about a Baxter-type personality.

Should Jim and Wendy have gone to the wedding at all?

Over the next few years, Baxter and Linda moved from state to state, living in trailer homes and apartments all over he place. In the five years they were married, they lived nearly 0 different places because Baxter couldn't hold onto a job.

Early on, we made up our minds to support their marriage nd do our best to help them succeed. We tried to encourage hem and pray for them. We sent each of them birthday ;ifts and money for their anniversary. We flew them home or the holidays on several occasions. In general, we tried o treat Baxter like one of our own children. Things were isually amiable during their visits, although Baxter would iot let Linda or their children stay in our home. He was eluctant for us to have time alone with Linda. And there was dways a tentativeness and guardedness on Linda's part when .he was with us. It was as if she knew Baxter was watching her.

What was Baxter really afraid of?

This is where my story becomes almost unbearable to tell ou. Jim passed away about 6 months ago, and I've been rying to hold everything together. On the morning of Linda's 29th birthday I called her and found out that she ιad seriously injured her knee while packing for another nove. Apparently, Baxter had lost yet another job and was out job hunting. He had left Linda at home to pack and :are for their two little girls, despite the fact that she was six nonths pregnant. Her knee was swollen, and she was in a lot of pain. Being a registered nurse for years, I strongly urged her :o go to the doctor to get it checked out, but she resisted, making excuses that they did not have health insurance and that Baxter didn't think it was necessary.

Did Linda need Baxter's permission to go to the hospital?

Two weeks later, Linda called me and told me she was having shortness of breath. At this point, the warning bells went off in my head as to the seriousness of her injury. I realized that a blood clot had probably dislodged from her knee and was now traveling up through her body. I begged her to call 911 and assured her that I would pay for the expense. She refused once again. The next day she called to say she was feeling clammy and miserable and that she was throwing up. I pleaded with her to go to the hospital. Her older sister called her and reiterated my plea. But Linda still refused to go.

Two days later, at 6:00 in the morning, my phone rang. Baxter's father was on the other end. He said coldly and with no emotion, "This is Herb. Linda is dead."

I experienced not only the pain and sorrow of losing a child but also sadness because it was all so unnecessary—and especially after being a widow for such a short time. My fragile heart felt as if it couldn't be any more broken. The grief I felt in the loss of Linda was complicated by my anger toward my abusive son-in-law. As details of Linda's death unfolded, I came to understand that the night before Linda died, she told Baxter that she was having chest pain and numbness in her arm. But he refused to allow her to go to the hospital.

He got up the next morning and left her for the entire day. It wasn't until he came home ten hours later that he found her dead. My two grand-babies were alone with their mother's lifeless body in the bathroom for ten hours until their father came home from work! Even then, he waited another three hours to call 911, choosing instead to pray over her body, for God to raise her from the dead. What a joke! The police launched an investigation in regard to suspected neglect of Linda by Baxter. There was not enough evidence to press charges.

> **Why didn't Baxter call Linda's family immediately after her death? How does Baxter's behavior compare with Philippians 2:3–4?**

The days that followed were nothing short of a nightmare. I immediately got on a plane to help with my granddaughters and to be there for Linda's burial. I was met with resistance from Baxter and his family when I offered to pay for the casket and flowers. They were planning to make her a casket out of lumber! I was overwhelmed with anger toward them. They didn't have the decency to consider anyone else's emotional needs but their own! This was just another expression of Baxter's self-centered, controlling, and abusive attitude we'd seen all along. Little had we known it would end up costing my daughter her life.

At one point, I confronted Baxter and told him that I held him responsible for Linda's death. In a cocky and flippant manner, he responded, "Well, God's grace is sufficient." His parents later told me that they supported Baxter's decision not to take her to the hospital because "the doctors couldn't have done anything to help her anyway." How I struggled with hatred toward them! And as if all of that wasn't bad enough, on the morning of Linda's memorial, Baxter found a poem I had written to read at the funeral. He told me he didn't want me to read it and refused to let me have any part in the service.

Now that those initial months of grieving have passed I realize that the next step is to forgive my son-in-law. I cannot change what has happened. My daughter is gone, but I know I can choose to forgive Baxter and allow the Lord to take away my resentment and bitterness toward him. I want nothing more than to be able to have a good and meaningful relationship with my granddaughters. He can be a very controlling and difficult father, so I want to be a spiritual influence in their life and a reminder of their mother to them. In order for that to happen, I must put the past behind, be forgiving and focus on my granddaughters.

Thanks for letting me share my story. — Wendy

I'll close this story with one general observation. Jim and Wendy illustrate how Christian "branches" draw amazing strength from Jesus Christ, the Vine. This is where Christian commitment and biblical application meet the road. Walking in Wendy's shoes would be a tough assignment, but she has God's power delivered to her through the Vine, allowing her to live with grace, love, and submission.

CHAPTER TWENTY-EIGHT

Unfruitful Branches

Let's be honest, Jim and Wendy were facing difficult waters with Linda long before she met Baxter. Her rebellion was already taking its toll on the family, and her unwise involvement with the B-man only added fuel to the fire. Jim and Wendy did everything they could to guide their daughter and protect her from Mr. Knucklehead, but she was so stubborn, self-willed, and foolish that she couldn't (or wouldn't) hear a word they said.

Frankly, many times parents are more concerned for their children than their children are for themselves. Parents long to see their children make wise choices, but often their children aren't nearly as interested in or concerned about those choices. A serious problem exists when a parent is willing to invest everything in a child's future and the child isn't willing to invest anything in their own future. Parents can encourage, counsel, or teach until they are blue in the face, but if their child doesn't care about his or her own well-being, rebellion is right around the corner. This was the problem with Linda. She didn't care as much about her future as her parents did.

If you have spent any time reading Proverbs, you can probably hear the words of King Solomon ringing in your ears right now:

> A wise son [or daughter] makes a father glad, but a foolish son [or daughter] is a grief to his mother. (Proverbs 10:1)

> A foolish son [or daughter] is a grief to his father. (Proverbs 17:25)

> A foolish son [or daughter] is destruction to his father. (Proverbs 19:13)

The author of Proverbs actually spent a lot of ink on the issue of rebellious children. He knew what he was talking about. He describes them as those who refuse parental oversight and counsel (Proverbs 13:1), despise their parents' instruction (Proverbs 15:5), and curse, mock, and dishonor their parents (Proverbs 30:11, 17; 19:26), leading to a life of great foolishness. They are foolish (Proverbs 17:25), disobedient and, just like a "bird hastens to the snare, so he does not know that it will cost him his life" (Proverbs 7:23).

Ponder that last verse for a minute, and you'll see its truth. When children start down the path of personal rebellion and indifference towards parents, their hearing is shut off and their understanding is minimized, limiting their ability to make wise choices. They become extra vulnerable to undesirable friends and potential partners. Linda's statement "I am going to do it anyway" tells it all. She was headed into a problematic relationship, unable to comprehend how serious it was because she had distanced herself from her parents and their counsel. This form of rebellion creates blind spots leading to very unwise choices. Absalom (2 Samuel 15:1–37), Eli's sons (1 Samuel 2:22–25), Samuel's sons (1 Samuel 8:3), and others point to the futility of rebellion and blind disobedience.

One might ask, "What was Mr. Knucklehead Baxter doing all this time?" I can assure you he wasn't encouraging Linda to take whatever time was necessary to understand her parents' concern. No, he was taking her side against Jim and Wendy, undermining them and belittling their opinions. This only reinforced Linda's rebellion against them. Instead of encouraging unity and trying to be a peacemaker, Baxter became a wedge that drove Linda farther away from her parents. You see, that's what abusers do—they do their best to isolate their victims from any other influence. Baxter was an abusive man who wanted Linda fully under his control. Between her rebellion and Baxter's controlling influence, Linda became separated from the protective counsel of her loving parents.

If you compare Baxter's handling of the situation to that of Jacob and his future father-in-law Laban in Genesis 29, the contrast is astonishing. Jacob loved Laban's daughter Rachel and desired to have her for his wife. But Laban wasn't quite ready for that to happen. The two men agreed that Jacob would serve Laban for seven years in exchange for Rachel. But Laban was a deceitful man and did a "bait and switch" on Jacob. At the end of the seven years, on Jacob's wedding night, he gave him his other daughter Leah instead! Jacob ended up working another seven years in order to marry Rachel. But the amazing thing is, during those 14 years (and even the years after them), Scripture never mentions anything about Jacob having an angry, controlling, or hateful attitude toward Laban. He patiently waited for his future father-in-law's approval and showed him honor, even though Laban was deceitful. All future sons-in-law could learn a lot from Jacob's patience and willingness to consider the desires of his in-law.

What's so ironic is Baxter and Linda were professing Christians. I underscore "professing" because they certainly didn't act in a biblical manner. They seemed to know something of the Bible but were "hearers" of the Word not "doers" of the Word. Recall Baxter's very trite use of Scripture following Linda's death: "Well, God's grace is sufficient." We might ask, what happened to Baxter's spiritual leadership and the sacrificial love for his wife and her family? Shouldn't he have encouraged Linda to "honor father and mother?" Shouldn't he set the example to "pursue the things which make for peace and the building up of one another" (Romans 14:19)? Shouldn't they have gone to Linda's parents before they went to church for worship in an attempt to reconcile their differences (Matthew 5:23–24)?

Thankfully there wasn't a total break in the relationship. Jim and Wendy knew their relationship with Linda was more important than fighting over Baxter. They did their best to help Linda understand what kind of person Baxter was, but she wanted no part of it. When they couldn't alter or slow down the trajectory of Baxter and Linda's relationship, maintaining their own relationship with Linda became the ultimate goal. This meant they had to accept Baxter's arrogance and controlling personality. To become angry, and to confront or challenge Baxter would only confirm his accusations against them. They would lose Linda forever, and they knew they couldn't handle that. They needed to be there for her and their future grandchildren.

Jim and Wendy's only option was to humbly (Luke 14:11, James 4:6), prayerfully, and strategically work with an undesirable son-in-law, a rebellious daughter, and a very rough situation. And they were able to maintain some kind of relationship with Linda, which Wendy kept up until Linda's untimely death. But if they hadn't been humble, careful, and strategic, that fragile relationship with Linda and Baxter could have been severed at any point. Had that happened, Wendy would never have been able to enjoy her grandchildren as she does today.

CHAPTER TWENTY-NINE

Bent But Not Broken

In the last chapter, I focused on Jim's and especially Wendy's efforts to maintain a relationship with Linda and Baxter, despite their rebellion and hostility. I want to delve a little deeper into how Wendy was able to do this. You see, as I reread their story, I ask myself what I would do in their situation. My impatience might take hold of me, and who knows what might happen. But that's why I'm so thankful for Jim and Wendy's patient example. They persevered in the tumultuous relationship with Linda and Baxter, and Wendy continues to stand tall amidst such trying times. This is only possible because she is trusting in God's divine plan, for her family and ultimately for His Glory.

Early in her story, Wendy states a couple of life principles that helped her face the storm head on. It's plain to see that trusting God was the spiritual GPS (Global Positioning System) that continued to lead her. She says, "I've grown to trust Him more." In Proverbs 3:5–6, the wise Solomon advises us to "trust in the Lord with all your heart and do not lean on your own understanding. In all your ways acknowledge Him, and He will make your paths straight." Throughout the Scriptures, we are encouraged to trust in the Lord for our well-being and God's glory. We must see our loving heavenly Father as being in charge of all of life's events. Remember God is sovereign, and we are just "clay in the Father's hand." "The thing molded will not say to the molder, 'Why did you make me like this,' will it? Or does not the potter have a right over the clay?" (Romans 9:20–21)

However, as Wendy says, "trusting God takes courage." It requires a certain relinquishing of our authority over a situation. In order for us to trust Him, God needs to be really big in our lives and we must be small. A spiritual upset arrives when our spiritual mindset says we, the parents, are "large and in charge" and God is small and unable to take care of our children. It's down in the trenches of a child's rebellion that we must trust in God, as the father of the Prodigal Son did in Luke 15. The Psalms encourage us over and over again to turn to the Lord, entrusting our very lives to Him, for He is our refuge and strength.

This is not always easy. Life is trying, children can seem impenetrable, solutions aren't that easy, and compromising is terribly hard. We know we should trust God implicitly in every area of our lives. But it's another thing entirely to trust Him with the lives of our children and whom they marry!

But I want to encourage you, God has a plan for you, your children, their spouses, and your grandchildren. And He is sovereignly in control of everything that goes on in your life and the lives of your family members. God isn't sitting distracted somewhere in heaven, wringing His hands and stressing out when difficulties come our way. Rather, He promises to use those challenges for our good and His glory. Rather than everyone getting frustrated, we need to let God be God. Our job is to apply Scripture to our lives, trusting in faith that God will complete His perfect plan in the lives of our children. It was this trust and faith that allowed Wendy to be patient and persevere in the face of such trials and difficulties.

Let me just say one more thing about trusting God. It doesn't mean passively sitting on the couch, watching the weekend football game, or knitting the grandchild a fancy sweater with an "I could not care less" attitude. Rather it's doing what a parent can do and giving the results up to God. Wendy is a perfect example of this. She trusted the Lord, but also fasted and prayed for God to help Linda. She also kept reaching out to them and invited them over for dinners. Jim and Wendy consistently affirmed their love to Linda and Baxter, tried to talk to them, and even gave them money for their honeymoon. All of this was an ongoing expression of love. Linda's rebellion and Baxter's hostility couldn't shake Wendy's trust in God. And her trust in Him was as an active trust, not just a passive trust that sits back and does nothing.

Too often God is the "800-pound spiritual gorilla" that we fail to see as our all-wise, all-powerful God who is present in our family life. He is there but seriously ignored as we go about trusting in our own efforts, relying on our own insights, and acting foolishly. As trust in God wanes, human determination, stubbornness, and self-justification accelerate, making possibilities for a healthy relationship a pipe dream.

CHAPTER THIRTY

Necessary Pruning

Throughout their story, we see Jim and Wendy demonstrate great restraint, even though at times the anger and hurt they felt must have seemed overwhelming. Miraculously, Wendy dealt with her feelings spiritually and trusted in Christ. They not only professed Christ, they lived Christ. On the other hand, Mr. Knucklehead Baxter and Linda professed to follow Christ but lived very selfishly. Professing to be a Christian can be a rather empty phrase if it isn't followed by godly attitudes and actions.

In Ephesians 4:1–3, Paul the apostle encourages us to "walk in a manner worthy of the calling . . . with all humility and gentleness, with patience, showing tolerance for one another in love, being diligent to preserve the unity of the Spirit in the bond of peace." My question is, shouldn't this teaching apply to sons- or daughters-in-law as well? Jim and Wendy tried desperately to live out the fruit of the Spirit (Galatians 5:22–23, "love, joy, peace, patience, kindness, goodness, faithfulness, gentleness, self-control") toward their child and son-in-law, but their efforts were not reciprocated by either Linda or Baxter. Instead, rebellion and intolerance marked Baxter and Linda's heartless disconnect with Jim and Wendy.

In contrast to the fruit of the Spirit, the apostle Paul describes the works of the flesh: "strife, jealousy, outbursts of anger, disputes, dissensions, factions, envying" (Galatians 5:19–21). These are all wicked and unchristian attitudes, and Baxter and Linda consistently displayed such attitudes and behavior toward her parents. How childish of Baxter and Linda to treat her parents with such disdain and self-centeredness. Proverbs 19:26 says a person who mistreats his father and mother (or in-laws) "is a shameful and disgraceful son [or daughter]."

When I think about Wendy's situation, the lack of consideration and respect from her own daughter, my heart goes out to her. Wendy and Jim devoted so much time and expense in training and bring up their children in the "discipline and instruction of the Lord" (Ephesians 6:4). How Wendy has endured is certainly a work of God's Spirit within her.

In contrast to a true follower of Christ, a person like Baxter is a dangerous snake in the grass, waiting to poison relationships. This poison comes out of his own personal insecurity, inflated ego, and lack of biblical Christlikeness and Christian character. Rather than being a peacemaker, working to draw

Linda and her family closer together, he became the enabler of hurt and division.

As I consider Wendy's story, 1 Corinthians 13 seems to be very descriptive of her whole situation. This might surprise you because you probably know that as the "love chapter" in the Bible. But let me explain.

I think Baxter's "religious" behavior falls under the first three verses. Before beginning to describe what love is and is not, Paul says,

> If I speak with tongues of men and angels . . . have the gift of teaching and know all mysteries and knowledge and have all faith . . . if I give all my possessions to the poor and even die as a martyr but *have not love*, I've become a clanging cymbal, nothing and unprofitable. (1 Corinthians 13:1–3; italics added)

It wouldn't matter if Baxter did some very "Christian" things. Without love, they are all meaningless and worthless. Snapshots of Baxter's self-centered attitudes and actions are quite apparent in the passage.

Now look at verses 4–7. When Paul describes what love is not, we can see those snapshots of Baxter's attitudes and actions.

> Love is patient, love is kind and is not jealous; love does not brag and is not arrogant, does not act unbecomingly; it doesn't seek its own, is not provoked, does not take into

account a wrong suffered, does not rejoice in unrighteousness, but rejoices with the truth; bears all things, believes all things, hopes all things, endures all things. (1 Corinthians 13:4–7)

Wendy's deep love for God and her commitment to His word provided the supernatural ability to continue reaching out in 1 Corinthians 13 love. It is easy to see her faith being lived out. She has lived acting upon Scripture. She is like the person who built his house on solid rock:

Everyone who hears these words of Mine and acts on them, may be compared to a wise man who built his house on the rock. And the rain fell, and the floods came, and the winds blew and slammed against that house [Wendy's house]; and yet it did not fall, for it had been founded on the rock. (Matthew 7:24–25)

When you consider the actions of Baxter, you'll readily see that his self-love was very sick, childish, and sinful. His behavior and attitudes are completely wrong and in need of Christ's intervention. He illustrates the foolish person who hears these words of [Christ] and does not act on them":

"[He] will be like a foolish man who built his house on the sand. The rain fell, and the floods came, and the winds blew and slammed against that house [Baxter's house]; and it fell—and great was its fall." (Matthew 7:26–27)

I'm looking out my window at a grapevine. There are branches that have grapes on them, but other branches are not producing any fruit and need to be pruned. Some of the branches are dead and should definitely be cut off. It is very easy to tell the difference.

The same is true of the Vine and the branches Jesus spoke of in John 15. Christ is the Vine, and people are the branches. Certain branches (Christians) bear fruit. Others (also Christians) produce some fruit, but not very much, so they need to be pruned. In fact, we all need to be pruned periodically by the Vinedresser, to help us produce more fruit! But there are some dead branches too. They are unbelievers, or professing Christians without real faith and no fruit. These dead branches will eventually be cut off from the Vine.

Baxter, Linda, Jim, and Wendy all professed to be Christians. But a mere profession is not evidence enough to indicate that someone is connected to the Vine. Bearing fruit is the only means whereby we can tell if a person is a live branch in need of pruning or a fruitful branch. Jesus Himself said, "You will know them by their fruits" (Matthew 7:20) There's no question that Jim and Wendy were attached to the Vine and abiding in the Vine. Baxter and Linda, however appear to be another story.

Part Eight
Safe and Unsafe People

CHAPTER THIRTY-ONE

Some Relationships Aren't Safe

J ust recently I went fishing with a friend I've known since junior high school (that's about 60 years ago). We splashed around the river laughing at one another, reminiscing, and catching fish for two days. It was a landmark time together.

Over the years, I've been blessed with many meaningful friendships through business, church, and ministry involvement. We've worked together, played together raised families together, and served God together. Some have been friends for decades. We've grown up from young whippersnappers into senior citizens. Looking back, I can see how we've grown spiritually together, prayed for each other been challenged by one another and wept over our failures. I praise God for so many wonderful folks who have touched my life.

These relationships are so precious because they are "safe. My own grandchildren have commented with surprise at how many friends Grandpa and Grandma have. And why shouldn't we? There are many wonderful "safe" people on this planet. Some of them are Christians, some of them are not. But they are still safe. In other words, they are easy to be with.

But here's where the "rub" comes. What happens when your son or daughter marries a person who suffers from internal emotional conflict and is an "unsafe" person? All of a sudden, you have a gigantic issue you can't get rid of. A destructive person who is very self-centered and filled with self-pity has joined your family. Now that's a problem.

The following is Jeff's story. He does a good job of explaining what it's like to interact with an unsafe person.

Jake and Allison met at work. They shared a cubical in the office, and both loved their jobs. That mutual interest led to a dating relationship. Jake was handsome and seemed like a nice guy. But when he professed to be a Christian, we had our doubts.

How is personal testimony validated?

Jake and Allison dated for ten months, and we tried our best to get to know him, but struggled to be at peace with their relationship. One of our concerns was his family background. Jake's parents were divorced when he was 6 years old. His father had remarried and divorced another couple times. (To our knowledge, neither of Jake's parents are Christians.) We talked openly with Allison about our concerns and even begged her to reconsider. But she was deadset on marrying Jake.

What kind of emotional baggage might Jake carry from his parents' divorce?

Once they were married, Jake dumped Christianity like a hot potato, stating he had never actually believed anything he claimed during the premarital counseling. That revelation was the start of a marriage characterized by godless control, manipulation, and criticism. Jake never negotiates or compromises, and everything must be done his way or there'll be hell to pay. He hates doing jobs around the house and blows his top if dinner isn't ready the minute he walks into the house. He's so selfish it's sickening.

Where do you think Jake's paranoia and need for control come from?

Even while he and Allison were dating, our relationship with Jake was strained; we were like polite strangers. I was hopeful things would change, but immediately after the wedding the lights of hope went out. Since then, our relationship with Jake has been either difficult or nonexistent. When there is communication, it is done through Allison. Jake will rarely speak to us. Whenever they come to visit Colorado, they always stay with Jake's mother, never with us. In the 8 years they've been married, Jake has been to our home once. Of course

llison makes excuses for Jake and we try to understand. She
ays he's very unsocial and has no friends, so I guess we're not
he only problem.

Why was Jake willing to have interaction with Jeff and his wife before the wedding but completely cut them off afterward?

Jake is very controlling of our interactions with the
randchildren. We can't even take them to the beach or for
bike ride. We haven't been allowed to babysit them, either.
During one of our visits, Jake became angry with me because
was apparently not being careful enough while playing
utside. Surely he knows a grandfather would never put his
randchild in jeopardy? But it's really not about that—it's
bout his need to control everything. I think he's envious of all
he fun we have with the grandchildren and is jealous of our
elationship with Allison. He can't stand to have Allison pay
ttention to us. Whenever we try to spend time with Allison,
ake always butts in. Allison feels caught between Jake and
s. She wants to be there for Jake and the children, but she
lso loves us (her parents) and wants to stay in touch.

Let me give you one more example of what it's like
o interact (or try to interact) with Jake. Not too long ago,
ny father (Allison's grandfather) died. We decided to share
portion of our inheritance with each of our children and
heir spouses. When we gave some of the money to Allison,
e did so with one stipulation. We wanted them to use the

money for a nice vacation rather than simply paying off bills. That's what Grandpa would want, and we thought it was a nice gesture. Well, within a day or two, Jake called to tell us how offended and angry he was because we had "told them how to spend the money." Once again, we tried to handle him with grace and love, but it's getting old fast.

> **How can Jeff and his wife make time with the grandchildren and Allison special in spite of Jake's attitude?**

I'm at the point where I don't even want to try anymore. How should I treat a person who has no appreciation or respect for me or my wife? He wants nothing to do with us. I want to do the right thing and I want their marriage to work out, but I am just so exhausted, angry, and frustrated by all of this. Would knocking him over the head with a 2x4 be helpful? Please help! — Jeff

---

There are many wonderful "safe" people on this planet. Some of them are Christians, some of them are not. But they are still safe. In other words, they are easy to be with.

CHAPTER THIRTY-TWO

Playing It "Safe"

Before Jeff's story, I described Jake as an "unsafe" person. The story gives you an idea, but let me explain what I mean by "safe" and "unsafe" people a bit more. It's an important subject to grasp for any kind of relationship, but it's especially relevant to our subject of difficult sons- and daughters-in-law.

Someone has rightfully said "you can choose your friends but not your relatives." You certainly can't choose your son or daughter-in-law; your child did that for you. Consequently, you must accept their idiosyncrasies, their eccentricities, and any unbiblical attitudes and actions. When a son- or daughter-in-law comes into your family, they bring with them their history, which in some cases might include all sorts of personal baggage.

Generally speaking, a toxic son- or daughter-in-law refuses any sort of counseling or biblical guidance. Another common trait is that they have very few (if any) long-term friendships. Often the only long-term relationships held by these troubled individuals are with their parents of origin. That's understandable because "blood is thicker than water." A dad or mom will tolerate their child's insane behavior, whereas friends (or in-laws) find it very difficult to be around them because they're "unsafe."

I use the term "unsafe" because that's a perfect description for a difficult son- or daughter-in-law. They're very "unsafe" to be around. So, what would a "safe" person be like?

We all would agree that Jesus is a safe Person, full of "grace and truth" (John 1:14). He unconditionally loves and accepts us without condemnation (Romans 8:1, Ephesians 4:32). Therefore, we might conclude that a person who is "safe" would love unconditionally and selflessly take an interest in another's personal life. Safe people are empathetic, concerned about others, and understand the needs of others (1 Corinthians 3:5). They encourage you to grow spiritually, resulting in an increased love for others. A safe person would be an example of Christlike character. He or she is the person everyone would love to have for a friend or a family member.

"Safe" friends and "safe" family members are like a breath of fresh air. They're transparent. They aren't afraid to admit weakness and are genuinely humble and trustworthy. You just feel better when you're around them. They help you reach your potential through their investment in you. Their laughter, humor, and kindness make life seem less difficult, less stressful, and less uncertain. Knowing they "have your back" is a great assurance. They are the type of good friend or relative who is "safe" to be around.

Safe people aren't perfect, but the description I just gave is how they usually act and treat others. How, then, would you describe an "unsafe" friend or family member? They are just the opposite—you don't feel comfortable around them; they talk about themselves most of the time; they are critical, judgmental, and condemning toward others; you'll seldom (if ever) hear them apologize for hurting your feelings, or for being insensitive or wrong; they are chronic "takers" instead of "givers."

While this isn't an exhaustive description, it should give you an idea of what an "unsafe" person is like. In fact, you can probably think of a few you know. "Unsafe" people can be difficult to spot initially. They can "fly under the radar" and disguise their character flaws for a while, but in time the truth surfaces and they are exposed. This is why "unsafe" people struggle to maintain relationships long term.

I borrow the terms "safe people" and "unsafe people" from Drs. Henry Cloud and John Townsend, in their book *Safe People*. Here are some telltale signs they list (along with my summary thoughts) that can make it easier to identify an "unsafe" person:

- "Unsafe people think they 'have it all together' instead of admitting their weaknesses."[1] This makes a person feel

---

[1] Henry Cloud and John Townsend, *Safe People: How to Find Relationships That Are Good for You and Avoid Those That Aren't* (Grand Rapids: Zondervan, 1995), 28–29

disconnected, beneath, weaker than, dependent, angry at the one who "has it all together" and needing to compete to reverse the role.

• "Unsafe people are religious instead of spiritual."[2] Rules give them power. Outward appearance is very important, but to be spiritual takes selflessness and sacrifice.

• "Unsafe people are defensive instead of open to feedback."[3] They always justify their actions against others and are never open to confrontation without getting defensive.

• "Unsafe people are self-righteous instead of humble."[4] An unsafe person doesn't admit sin because they think they are better than those who commit sin. Like the hypocrites, they judge others but cannot admit to their own flaws.

• "Unsafe people only apologize instead of changing their behavior."[5] They never repent of wrongdoing.

• "Unsafe people avoid working on their problems instead of dealing with them."[6] How can they work on problems they deny having?

• "Unsafe people demand trust, instead of earning it."[7] When you're uncomfortable with a person, you don't trust them. Trust must be earned by the investment of one person into the life of another. It can't be demanded.

---

[2]Ibid., 29–30, [3]Ibid., 30–31 [4]Ibid., 31–32, [5]Ibid., 32–34, [6]Ibid., 34, [7]Ibid., 35–36,

- "Unsafe people believe they are perfect instead of admitting their faults."[8] This is the basic problem with "unsafe" people. They use their work, family, abilities, or religion to project a false image of perfection. They will fight, point fingers, and blame others in order to appear blameless.

- "Unsafe people blame others instead of taking responsibility."[9] Rather than be responsible before God for their sinfulness, they assume the "victim" role and blame other people, their past, God, sin, or anything else. They are filled with excuses for bad behavior and bad attitudes.

- "Unsafe people lie instead of telling the truth."[10] Truth-telling is too intimidating to an unsafe person, so they live in a state of perpetual denial.

I think it's safe to say that all of the toxic in-laws described in this book are "unsafe" people. What do you do if you end up with an "unsafe" family member? Knowing what to do is a difficult proposition. I think it's wise to understand the limitations of an "unsafe" person, so your expectations become more realistic. Don't try to push the relationship too hard or it will be like "pushing a rope uphill."

Lowering your expectations is one way to keep yourself safe around an "unsafe" person. Another way is to install some protective boundaries (like staying in a hotel when visiting).

---

[8]Ibid., 36, [9]Ibid., 36–37, [10]Ibid., 37–38

Focus on keeping yourself safe from them in order to maintain the relationship. But do so not in a way that pushes them away or discards the relationship. Always remember you might be the closest they ever get to a truly "safe" Christian who loves them unconditionally as Jesus would.

Also, one more reminder: Even safe people make mistakes and act like "unsafe" people. We are sinners, after all.[11] Here is what Dr. Cloud and Dr. Townsend add after their list of the traits of unsafe people:

> When you are measuring someone's character, look at these traits in terms of degree. Everyone lies at some time or in some way. But not everyone is a pathological liar. Look for degrees of imperfection. If a person seems willing to change, forgive him graciously and work with him. But if he resists you, proceed with caution.[12]

---

[11]Ibid., 38, [12]Ibid.,39

CHAPTER THIRTY-THREE

Conclusion

Before we finish this book, let's do a little review. Reading these stories can certainly leave us a bit discouraged. We can feel the parents' helplessness, despair, and agony of heart while a son- or daughter-in-law brings havoc into their lives. It's like having an angry bull in your china closet—what a mess! I won't apologize for being a bit hard on destructive sons- or daughters-in-law in this book. Their actions and attitudes not only make me angry, but are also downright wrong and very exhausting to cope with.

When you consider the sinfulness of every person on this planet, it's no surprise that relationships are often treacherous. It's frightening to consider how easy it is for us as parents or in-laws to become part of the problem rather than part of the solution. After all, we are sinners as well. If we harbor sinful attitudes, they can turn into sinful actions like "strife, jealousy, angry tempers, disputes, slanders, gossip arrogance, disturbances… impurity, immorality and sensuality" (2 Corinthians 12:20–21).

To say these sinful behaviors aren't in the hearts of Christian parents would be a lie of the devil himself. It humbles me to confess the struggles present in my own heart. Often my own responses to difficult relationship issues aren't helpful and only cause more hurt feelings. In James 3:13–18 the practical apostle addresses these types of sinful attitudes, along with their sinful results, and gives us some timely counsel:

> Who among you is wise and understanding? Let him show by his good behavior his deeds in the gentleness of wisdom. But if you have bitter jealousy and selfish ambition in your heart, do not be arrogant and so lie against the truth. This wisdom is not that which comes down from above, but is earthly, natural, demonic. For where jealousy and selfish ambition exist, there is disorder and every evil thing. But the wisdom from above is first pure, then peaceable, gentle, reasonable, full of mercy and good fruits, unwavering, without hypocrisy. And the seed whose fruit is righteousness is sown in peace by those who make peace.

I would suggest you pay close attention to the differences between the two types of wisdom. When handling a difficult son or daughter-in-law, be extremely careful about which type of wisdom you apply because one is from above (notice the attributes of this spiritual wisdom) and the other is from below (notice the attributes of this demonic wisdom).

One of the reasons for writing this book was to let parents know that they are not alone. Many families suffer from these difficult or toxic in-laws. If you're in such a situation, here's my challenge to you: it is up to you to set an example of being patient, respectful, and humble. Just because you're mistreated, ignored, accused, etc. doesn't mean it is okay for you to do the same. Because a toxic son- or daughter-in-law is rude, inconsiderate, distant, or just plain impossible doesn't give you the right to respond impatiently, disrespectfully, angrily or vengefully. You must endeavor to apply the "wisdom from above," not the "wisdom from below" to your situation.

Let's apply this "wisdom from above" or the "gentleness of wisdom" to what we've learned about managing your relationship with a troublesome son- or daughter-in-law. I want to direct these concluding comments to each respective person:

1. Parent: Let me just say I have the highest respect for you, whether you're married or a single parent, young or old. You work your magic in the difficult environment of home life. You're not perfect, but you are there 24/7, trying to do the job God has entrusted to you. Sure, there have been distractions and countless goof-ups, but you've bounced back, sacrificing for your children, teaching them as best as you can and training them to live skillfully, with discernment and reverence for God. You are examples of what it looks like when the "wisdom from above" is applied to life. Oh, there have been failures along the way when "throwing in the towel" seemed like the better option. But you are spiritually resilient, always willing to confess your shortcomings, repent, and try to do better. As the old song says, you "take a deep breath… pick yourself up… dust yourself off… and start all over again."[1]

You've invested in your children, and now they're ready to tackle the world (or they will be soon). Way to go! Now you must let them go and then find new ways to encourage, guide, and exhort your adult child. They have left the nest—maybe too early or maybe too late—and the way you parent will be drastically different. At least, it certainly should be! The "wisdom from above" will guide you in this new adventure.

2. Father- or Mother-In-Law: You've entered into a whole different arena and frankly, you might not be ready for the transition that will need to take place. Buckle your seatbelt because the ride can get very bumpy, and it's pretty long. When your child looks at you and how you have raised them, you hope that he or she has confidence that, with God's help, they can accept the challenges of adulthood, and hopefully honor God in the process. If everyone involved will simply apply the "wisdom from above," which includes being "peaceable, full

---

[1]"Pick Yourself Up," composed by Jerome Kern, lyrics by Dorothy Fields, 1936.

of mercy... gentle," it will provide a seedbed for producing spiritual fruit in your family relationships.

But let me remind you: as a loving father- or mother-in law, knowing your place will have a drastic effect on outcomes If you're too opinionated, pushy, controlling, or manipulative trouble will appear on the horizon. Heed the "wisdom from above," which will encourage you to be "peaceable, gentle reasonable, full of mercy" (James 3:17). Avoid the wisdom from below, which displays itself in "jealousy and selfish ambition." The spirit of "my way or the highway" will bring grievous consequences. Always remember that adult relationships are very fragile, especially those between you and your son- or daughter-in-law. If you want to have a smooth time and eliminate as many bumps as possible be sure to apply the "wisdom from above."

Let me caution you that being grounded in sound "wisdom from above" doesn't necessarily negate the suffering and tribulation that will come your way through the evil efforts of a toxic son- or daughter-in law. Take a look at Peter in Acts 4 if you need confirmation. Peter believed God and was committed to following Him, and yet he was being persecuted consistently. If God is sovereign (and indeed He is), then experiencing suffering and heartache are part of His divine work in our lives, and He will use it for our good and His glory Keep in mind, "God causes all things to work together for good (Romans 8:28) and "we also exult in our tribulations, knowing that tribulation brings about perseverance ... character ... and hope" (Romans 5:3–4).

I'm truly sorry if your child has married a difficult son- or daughter-in-law. You didn't want it to happen like this, but some things are out of your control. As I've tried to communicate in this book, you're in a very awkward spot—one of those "damned if you do or damned if you don't" spots. It's really like walking through a minefield filled with explosives, not knowing where it's safe to step.

However, let's remind ourselves that God is with us moment by moment even in these tough transitions and trials. The psalmist tells us that while our "flesh and heart" may fail, "God is the strength" of our hearts and our "portion forever" (Psalm 73:26). I've been an eyewitness to the daily struggles fathers- and mothers-in-law have endured. At the same time, I've watched as they live out their biblical convictions with confidence knowing "that He who began a good work in you will perfect it until the day of Christ Jesus" (Philippians 1:6). Frankly, I find their faithful obedience to God's promises very encouraging.

Consider, then, the "peaceable, gentle, reasonable" means of acting and communicating as your pathway forward. The "wisdom from above" is always the preferred way to live in harmony with one another and to glorify God in the process. As I've repeated throughout this book, remember to smile, keep your mouth shut, and pray a lot because "time is on your side." Applying the "wisdom from above" effectively will help minimize unwanted explosions.

3. Adult Son or Daughter: I really want you to better understand the transition Dad and Mom embark on when you bring your boyfriend or girlfriend into the family mix. It might surprise you but your parents are very proud of you and really want the best for your life, including your love life. Since they've gotten some experience from the School of Hard Knocks, spotting the red lights or warning lights of unhealthy relationships can come pretty naturally for your parents. If you'll let them, they can help you understand many ins and outs of love relationships. Just a word of caution: when you marry, be very careful to maintain a relationship with your parents. Don't allow your spouse to turn you against them using "wisdom from below," full of "jealousy and selfish ambition." That isn't healthy. Rather strive to be a person who is "peaceable, gentle, reasonable, full of mercy and good fruits," exemplifying the "wisdom from above," and encourage your spouse to do the same.

One other thing: if you're presently unmarried, let me emphasize again the importance of premarital counseling, and within that, discussion about "How to interface with parents and in-laws after the wedding in a Christlike fashion." Many love relationships would have a better foundation if someone intercepted the hurtful attitudes, selfish intentions, and unbiblical responses directed towards parents or a future father- or mother-in-law before the wedding day.

Maybe you and your fiancé are a bit uncomfortable talking over personal matters with your dad or mom. I certainly understand that, and it may even be unwise for your parents or your future in-laws to do so. So find an outside person to communicate with. Maybe your pastor, mentor, or a friend would be a good choice. They'll be there for you, to help mature your relationship with that special person you intend to marry. Whomever you choose for premarital counseling, their good counsel can help you understand your independence as newlyweds, and at the same time you'll learn how to respect and balance the needs of other family members, especially those of your parents and your in-laws. As a new couple, you can "leave and cleave" to one another and at the same time value, respect, and honor extended family relationships.

The Bible clearly states, "Children. . . honor your father and mother (which is the first commandment with a promise), so that it may be well with you, and that you may live long on the earth" (Ephesians 6:1–3). This certainly applies to young children, but I've learned it also applies to adult children, whether single or married. Showing honor and respect for our parents at any age is very honorable and an essential Christian attribute. And it seems reasonable that the spirit of this great command should apply to your father-in-law and mother-in-law also. This requires "wisdom from above" in action.

4. Sons- and Daughter-In-Law: You are the reason for this book. For a long time, I've wanted to tackle the problem of difficult sons- and daughters-in-law, who dismiss valuable relationships using the "wisdom from below" through "jealousy and selfish ambition." They tend to manipulate, control and abuse their spouse and father- and mother-in law for their own selfish ends. Make no mistake—some of you are wonderful sons- and daughters-in-law who are a real blessing to your extended families. Let me just say, on behalf of your parents and your in-laws, thank you for acting with the "wisdom from above" and for seeking to build meaningful family relationships that honor Christ!

However, if you're one of the toxic and destructive sons- or daughters-in-law out there, and you happen to read this book, here is what I want to say to you. Right now, you are living according to the "wisdom from below" that manifests itself in "disorder and every evil thing." Living this way will bring much suffering into your life. In fact, it probably already has. The Psalmist says "the way of the treacherous is hard" (Proverbs 13:15) and "the treacherous will be caught by their own greed" (Proverbs 11:6) and "he who pursues evil will bring about his own death" (Proverbs 11:19). Living a life of self-focus has serious consequences. And the Bible gives us plenty of examples of such self-absorbed people:

- Samson's love interest Delilah, who was filled with selfishness and sought to undermine him

- Hosea's wife Gomer, who was self-absorbed and ignored the marital covenant by committing adultery

- Ananias' wife Sapphira, who participated in a corrupt, selfish, and ultimately deadly financial scheme

- Abigail's husband Nabal, who was a worthless man and a self-centered drunk

- Saul, the first king of Israel, whose self-focus caused insecurity, severe depression, and insane outbursts of anger

- Diotrephes of 3 John, a self-righteous man who loved to be first, didn't listen to others, spoke awful words, and was always judgmental and critical of others (even the apostles!)

Imagine what these men and women would be like as a son- or daughter-in-law. I can make an educated guess, because I've seen many like them come through my office. Do any of their traits hit "too close to home" for you? If so, it's time to make serious changes in your life. Living a self-absorbed life based on the "wisdom from below" will only bring heartbreak to you and those around you. The only way to break away from a life of self-centeredness—including self-focus, self-will, self-righteousness, self-defensiveness, and self-pity—is to realign your attitudes, words, actions, and relationships to the Bible.

If you profess to have faith in Jesus Christ as your Savior, you must allow your life to pass through the Bible, as it were, and be sanctified and changed by its teaching. God will help you through the enablement of the Holy Spirit who dwells within you.

However, you might not be a Christ-follower. Becoming a Christian is a very simple proposition. Since Jesus died on the cross for us (Romans 5:8, "God demonstrates His own love toward us, in that while we were yet sinners, Christ died for us"), all that is necessary is for you to receive Jesus as your personal Savior (John 1:12, "As many as received Him, to them He gave the right to become children of God, even to those who believe in His name") and turn away from your self-centered lifestyle. Then, and only then, will you experience a new way of approaching life by replacing evil attitudes and behaviors with a Christ-honoring respect for others (see 2 Corinthians 5:17, "If anyone is in Christ, he is a new creature; the old things passed away; behold, new things have come").

I'll close with this. Whether you're a parent, a father- or mother-in-law, a son or daughter, or a son- or daughter-in-law, you must break away from a self-centered life. That is the only way to have any hope of changing toxic, dysfunctional relationships. And it's something all parties involved must do. I beg all of you to experience the joy of knowing Jesus Christ as your personal Savior. Memorize and practice the apostle Paul's great teaching in Philippians 2:1–5:

Therefore if there is any encouragement in Christ, if there is any consolation of love, if there is any fellowship of the Spirit, if any affection and compassion, make my joy complete by being of the same mind, maintaining the same love, unified in spirit, intent on one purpose. Do nothing from selfishness or empty conceit, but with humility of mind regard one another as more important than yourselves; do not merely look out for your own personal interests, but also for the interests of others. Have this attitude in yourselves which was also in Christ Jesus.

Additional Resources
from Doyle Roth

These books are available through your favorite bookseller or through the publisher.

www.LewisandRoth.com

800.477.3239 (USA) | 719.494.1800 (International)

Oops! I Forgot My Wife:
A Story of Commitment as Marriage and
Self-Centeredness Collide

A marriage book for those who don't like marriage books!

Through humor, Biblical instruction and story, this book will help your marriage. Told through an exchange of emails, *Oops! I Forgot My Wife* follows the adventures and misfortunes of a guy who is so bad at husbanding that he wakes up one morning on the brink of divorce. Only then does he learn what it really means to "love your wife as Christ loves the church."

A discussion guide is also available, making this a valuable tool for group study.

"Roth...uses Scripture skillfully and liberally in teaching about marriage. The book...gives sound scriptural advice that is realistic and useful... [He] presents truth that many men would not read if it came in too fine and fancy a package. The story is intense enough to keep the reader reading through the book to learn of each development." — Elece Hollis, christianbookpreviews.com

Oops! I Forgot My Wife (Paperback)
Oops! I Forgot My Wife (Abridged, Audio CDs)
Oops! I Forgot My Wife Discussion Guide

Oops! We Forgot the Kids
A Story of Relationships as Parenting and
Self-Centeredness Collide

Thousands of couples have read Doyle Roth's *Oops!
I Forgot My Wife*. Now the subject is parenting. Once
again, you'll think he's sneaking a peek at your
family! Doyle's strategy is much the same: combine
situations from his decades in family counseling into
one engaging story, have the characters involved discuss
ffective parenting principles via email, add the practical "how tos" and season
all with humor and solid counsel from the Scriptures.

illed with down-to-earth advice, humor, an biblical instruction, *Oops!
'e Forgot the Kids* is sure to bring you a deeper appreciation of your family
and some hints on making it even better. (Not perfect, just better!)